CONTENTS

THE SECRETS ARE WITHIN YOU 9

How to Prepare Your Deck for Use **12**
How to Do a Reading with *The Tarot of Secrets* **14**
How to Do Magical and Spiritual Work with *The Tarot of Secrets* **20**

THE CARDS

0. The Fool **26**
1. The Magician **30**
2. The High Priestess **34**
3. The Empress **38**
4. The Emperor **42**
5. The Hierophant **46**
6. The Lovers **50**
7. The Chariot **54**
8. Strength **58**
9. The Hermit **62**
10. Wheel of Fortune **66**
11. Justice **70**

12. The Hanged **74**
13. Death **78**
14. Temperance **82**
15. The Devil **86**
16. The Tower **90**
17. The Star **94**
18. The Moon **98**
19. The Sun **102**
20. Judgment **106**
21. The World **110**

Ace of Vases **114**
Two of Vases **118**
Three of Vases **122**
Four of Vases **126**
Five of Vases **130**
Six of Vases **134**
Seven of Vases **138**
Eight of Vases **142**
Nine of Vases **146**
Ten of Vases **150**
Princess of Vases **154**
Knight of Vases **158**
Queen of Vases **162**
King of Vases **166**

Ace of Wands **170**
Two of Wands **174**
Three of Wands **178**
Four of Wands **182**

Five of Wands **186**
Six of Wands **190**
Seven of Wands **194**
Eight of Wands **198**
Nine of Wands **202**
Ten of Wands **206**
Princess of Wands **210**
Knight of Wands **214**
Queen of Wands **218**
King of Wands **222**

Ace of Swords **226**
Two of Swords **230**
Three of Swords **234**
Four of Swords **238**
Five of Swords **242**
Six of Swords **246**
Seven of Swords **250**
Eight of Swords **254**
Nine of Swords **258**
Ten of Swords **262**
Princess of Swords **266**
Knight of Swords **270**
Queen of Swords **274**
King of Swords **278**

Ace of Coins **282**
Two of Coins **286**
Three of Coins **290**
Four of Coins **294**

Five of Coins **298**
Six of Coins **302**
Seven of Coins **306**
Eight of Coins **310**
Nine of Coins **314**
Ten of Coins **318**
Princess of Coins **322**
Knight of Coins **326**
Queen of Coins **330**
King of Coins **334**

ABOUT THE AUTHOR **341**

ABOUT THE ARTIST **343**

THE SECRETS ARE WITHIN YOU

THERE ARE SECRETS HERE. Deep secrets. Timeless secrets. Secrets that will fascinate you, connect you with a formidable current of universal wisdom, and renovate your world.

These secrets are not imparted through words. They are not shown to you through the images. Their conveyance is not so straightforward as that. If it were that easy to procure the secrets, everyone would know them, and they wouldn't be secrets at all.

These precious enigmas and subtle formularies transmute the tin of everyday experience and the lead of oppressive challenges into a fountain of spiritual gold.

If you'd like to learn them, you're in luck. You're in the right place at the right time. Approach this deck with the earnest desire of the Magician, the patient focus of the High Priestess, and the limitless enthusiasm of the Fool.

Ask questions. Look for answers. Contemplate the images and let the words speak to you. In the moment, you will gain clarity. Over time, you will internalize the knowledge of the alchemists and the wisdom that echoes through the halls of eternity.

The secrets are within you, just as they are in the soil, the clouds, the oceans, and the stars. Through the interface of your attention, the images are the elixir; the words are the catalyst. This shimmering formula will spiral into you like a double helix of understanding, an infusion of your own transcendent DNA.

The first 22 cards (0 to 21) comprise the Major Arcana: The Fool (Card 0), journeys from all possibilities, through the ups and downs of experience, to the realized potential and lived experience of The World (Card 21). Then, the Fool finds himself back at the beginning. The same person is in the same place, but both have changed. And so, the cycle begins again.

The remaining cards are the Minor Arcana, which are divided into Vases, Wands, Swords, and Coins. These are the four elements, respectively: water, fire, air, and earth. Each numbered card (Ace to 10) is an aspect of the element in narrative. Each court card (princess, knight, queen, and king) is a human or a human dynamic that appears somewhere in your life or the situation at hand. It may be you, it may be someone else, and it may be an archetype or quality that is relevant in some significant way.

Again, each element journeys through the cycle, differentiating through various seasons and stages, and finds itself once again back at the Ace, but on a different layer of the spiral: the same but also different.

Tarot always tells a story. It shows you the themes and narratives that are showing up for you at any given time. It is comforting to know that while particulars are always unique, the core of what we experience is not. We are all human beings, having the human-being experience. Countless have had such experiences before, and countless will again.

If time is a circle and not a line, all of this is happening all the time.

As drops of the same ocean of timeless consciousness, we can tap into the vital resonance of collective understanding.

In seeing the archetypes and motifs through working with *The Tarot of Secrets*, you will gain a foothold on what is happening, and you will be empowered to proceed with an accelerated perspective.

Living wisdom waits for you. Begin where you are. Dive into the deep well of universal insight and move with the sweeping current of positive change.

HOW TO PREPARE YOUR DECK FOR USE

Here is a simple blessing ritual to align your personal energy with the energy of the deck and to prepare it for the clearest possible readings and most effective spiritual work.

First, set a mood. Light a candle (and perhaps some incense) or go outside somewhere calming and uplifting where you won't be disturbed. Play ambient instrumental music with binaural beats or hypnotic drumming and flute, through headphones, earbuds, or a speaker.

Place the cards before you on an altar or cloth. Relax with your spine straight in a comfortable way. Close your eyes and take some deep, conscious breaths. Then, allow your breath to be natural, but keep your awareness on the inhale and exhale until you feel calm, centered, and clear.

Pick up the deck and hold it in both hands. Close your eyes again and feel the energy of the cards. Also, direct your own personal energy into the cards. This is very much like holding hands. You offer support and receive support, through your hands, in a continuous loop. Breathe and feel yourself merging with the essence and personality of the deck.

Say a simple prayer of thanks for this auspicious moment, when you have crossed paths with this sacred body of wisdom that will lead you back to the oceanic field of cosmic intelligence that has been yours since the beginning of time.

Now, when you are ready, with curiosity and enjoyment, look at each card in turn. Simply soak in the images, noticing any sparks of interest and fascination, and feeling the feelings they evoke. There is no need to interpret anything or understand the card meanings in a linear or conscious way. This is simply about taking in the images, noticing what arises within you, and appreciating what you see.

When you've gazed, at least briefly, at every image in the deck, hold it in both hands again and express gratitude one more time. Then, shuffle the deck a few times and set it back down.

You can store your deck in the box it came in, or perhaps you'd prefer to store it in a special box or drawstring bag. If you'd like, you can place a clear quartz crystal point on top of your deck when it's not in use, to keep it charged up and hold the energy in place.

HOW TO DO A READING WITH *THE TAROT OF SECRETS*

To perform a reading with *The Tarot of Secrets*, you may like to create a mood first, as you did in the section above (i.e., by lighting a candle and possibly incense or finding a relaxing place outside and playing some ambient music). But you don't need to wait until this is possible before you can do a reading. You can work with this deck anytime and anywhere you like, provided you can relax your body and focus your mind.

First, choose a card spread. (You can select one from the section below or elsewhere.)

Once you have a spread in mind, hold the deck in both hands. Relax, breathe, and settle in.

Ask your question or focus on the issue you'd like guidance on. Yes or no questions are not helpful. Instead, phrase your question in an open-ended way, like:

- What do I need to know about [this situation]?
- How can I best move forward if I want to experience [this outcome]?
- Please give me insight into my relationship with [this person].
- How can I call back my power and regain my confidence?
- What guidance will help align me with prosperity and success?
- How can I make the most of [this enterprise or endeavor]?
- How can I best approach [this opportunity, challenge, or goal]?

- What might I expect if I [make this choice or take this action]?

Once you've phrased your question, shuffle the deck until you intuitively feel like stopping. (Whatever moment you choose will be correct.)

Next, cut the deck once or twice, using your left hand. Reassemble the deck and place the cards in the spread of your choice, image side up, taking the first cards off the top.

Be sure to gaze at the cards and let their imagery speak directly to your intuition before you turn to the corresponding pages in this book.

Be aware that some guidance will be obvious to you right away. Other aspects of the guidance, or in some readings, the wisdom will—through conscious or subconscious means—subtly penetrate your awareness throughout the day. It may even present itself to you in your dreams, or dawn on you at the moment you awake. Be curious and patient, knowing that if you ask your question in earnest and pay attention to the cards you receive, you will not fail to receive the guidance that will be most helpful to you, just when you need it most.

A word on reversals: reversals add an extra layer of possible meaning to each card. You may or may not choose to incorporate reversals in your readings. If you do, shuffle your cards in such a way that some will appear right-side up and some will appear upside down.

At the end of each card description in this guidebook, you will see a list of potential meanings and messages for each card when it appears upside down (or reversed).

If you don't want to use reversals, shuffle your cards in such a way that they always remain face up.

Following are five options for card spreads you might like to use for your readings.

ONE-CARD READING

This is an excellent spread to choose when you are in a hurry, or want immediate and obvious insight into any situation or challenge. You may like to use a one-card reading to draw a "card of the day" for general guidance on the day ahead.

After shuffling and cutting the deck as described above, simply draw the first card off the top and then consider how the card applies.

The card may characterize a relationship or dynamic in a way that brings necessary clarity, or it may offer instruction on how to proceed.

THREE-CARD READING

A three-card spread offers slightly more dimension and complexity.

Shuffle, cut, and then lay out the cards from left to right in a straight line of three.

Card One relates to the past or the foundations of the situation.

Card Two shows what's happening now.

Card Three characterizes the future.

The third card is not set in stone but is there to help you see the direction in which you're currently moving. If you'd like a different outcome, choose to relate to the present differently than you're doing now. You may already know how to do this, but for more insight on how to move forward, ask another question, and do another reading with any spread of your choice. (Before you shuffle for that one, remember to put the three cards from this reading back in the deck.)

FOUR-CARD READING

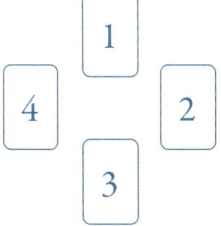

A four-card reading provides a sturdy base for wise action by illuminating the elemental dynamics at work.

Orient yourself so you are facing east. After shuffling and cutting the deck as described above, fashion a simple diamond shape, with Card One at the top of the spread, Card Two to the right, Card Three at the bottom and Card Four on the left.

Card One is the air element. It represents ideas and thoughts.
Card Two is the fire element. It sheds light on passions and desires for action.
Card Three is the water element: the currents of emotion and creativity that run through this situation.
Card Four is the earth element: practical matters, the solid ground beneath your feet, and the concrete actions that will help you succeed.

SEVEN-CARD READING

If you have a little more time, this spread is a classic for gaining insight and contemplating the best way to proceed.

Shuffle, cut once or twice, and lay out seven cards, left to right, with Card One on the left and Card Seven on the right.

Cards One, **Two**, and **Three** are like the three-card spread above: past, present, and future.
Card Four is advice: how to approach the situation and what to consider when deciding what to do.
Card Five is the dynamics at work: the people, places, things, and lessons that are present.

Card Six provides insight into the nature of the obstacles, roadblocks, or hidden challenges you may encounter.

Card Seven is the outcome if things proceed along the path they are on now. Much like in card three (the future card), this can be changed if you change the way you relate to the situation based on what you've learned from the reading.

HOW TO DO MAGICAL AND SPIRITUAL WORK WITH *THE TAROT OF SECRETS*

You need not employ a spread to receive guidance, wisdom, and support from *The Tarot of Secrets*. You can work directly with cards of your choosing to create positive change in your consciousness and your world.

You can follow your intuition for how to do this, but here are some ideas to get you started.

ASK THE QUEENS

Pull the four queens out of the tarot deck. Place the Queen of Swords to the east of you, the Queen of Wands to the south of you, the Queen of Vases to the west of you, and the Queen of Coins to the north of you.

Sit in the center of the queens, facing east.

Relax, take some deep breaths, and speak aloud your question. You may also describe a challenge or issue you'd like guidance on, as if you are indeed speaking to four wise queens. For example, perhaps you'd like more confidence, or maybe you'd like to know what to do about a particular relationship or business opportunity. Tell the queens all the ins and outs of what you are feeling.

Now, gaze at the Queen of Swords. Look at her image and let her speak her wisdom to you. Read her card description and notice what guidance stands out. Next, face south. Gaze at the Queen of Wands and repeat. Follow up with the same process facing west with the Queen of Vases and then facing north with the Queen of Coins.

You may like to jot down or summarize your insight in a journal or notebook.

THE STAR OF HEALING

To speed physical or emotional healing, pull the Star card out of the deck. Place it on your existing altar or create a simple altar using it as a focal point. Add a candle, perhaps some incense, and a healing crystal of your choice such as an aventurine, a clear quartz, or a blue lace agate.

Light the candle. Relax, breathe, and gaze at the image as you allow its renewing magic to shift your vibration and affect healing on all levels. As you look at the card and read its description, notice anything that stands out to you and take note of any specific guidance you intuitively receive.

THE HERMIT ILLUMINATES

Let's say you'd like to gain insight into your own desires or motivations, but you don't have the time or resources to take a solitary weekend retreat. Instead, pull the Hermit card out of the deck. Relax and gaze at the image on the card. Imagine you are going within, shutting out the noise and the distractions of the outside world.

Now, look deeply. What answer is there for you? What is it that you already know, but you didn't know you knew? Relax into silence until you gain the clarity and motivation you seek.

These are just three examples of the type of magical and spiritual work you can do with *The Tarot of Secrets*. But feel free to get creative. Ask the kings instead of the queens. Heal with Temperance instead of the Star. Gain insight with the High Priestess instead of the Hermit. You might ask Justice for help with a legal battle, or Strength to guide you in standing up for what you know is right.

If there's a card or subset of cards (like the knights or the aces) that speaks to you for any reason or purpose, work with it — even if you don't understand yet precisely why you're drawn to it. Look at it. Read about it. Sit with it. Journal about it. Light a candle, gaze at it, and invite it in.

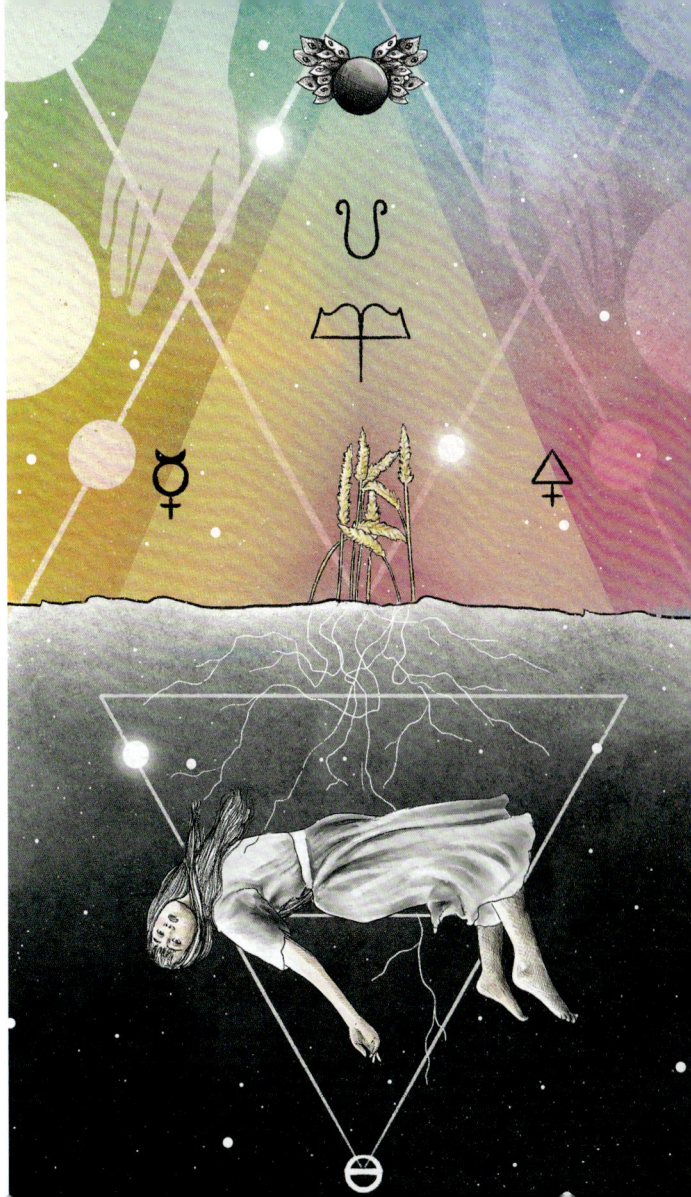

THE CARDS

0. THE FOOL
PURE POTENTIAL

GUIDANCE

There is unlimited potential here. Be bold and move forward without worrying, overthinking, or even needing a solid plan. A lucky break and an auspicious adventure are in store.

Indeed, the Fool reminds you that the whole universe is available to you, and all the transformative power, synchronicity, and magic contained therein.

You can't learn without making mistakes, and you'll limit your possibilities if you stay with what you already know. So, blunder awkwardly and valiantly into the unknown, and you will enlist the assistance of the gods, the angels, and all the stars in the sky.

DYNAMICS

The Fool is not foolish. Rather than seeking to master their domain, they seek to merge with it utterly, and swirl their personal magic into the primordial, kaleidoscopic mix. In so doing, they become one with the cosmic dance, and the cosmic dance endlessly, generously buoys their efforts and synchronizes their movements to the transcendent melody and beat.

While there are certainly times when it's appropriate to wait, plan, and meticulously get your foundations in place, this is not how the Fool rolls. Rather, the Fool gives very little thought to the form their path will take, much preferring to flow with whatever happens and learn as they go.

Rebirth, new beginnings, and splendid opportunities await you: they are in the clouds, the heavens, all around you in the landscape and ether, and beneath your very feet. But to access them, you must let go of caution, surrender overattachment to your ego, be willing to fail spectacularly, and dive into the cauldron of the glorious unknown.

Beautiful possibilities await you. But you can only receive them by letting go of needing to know when they will appear, how they will find you, or just what they will look like when they arrive.

Humbly admit that you know nothing, and the power of everything will be made available to you. This is the quality of magic that is sometimes called "beginner's luck."

S E C R E T S

The Fool is the first card, but not card number one. The Fool's number is zero: the vast, open emptiness in which everything arises and to which everything returns. Indeed, every card in the tarot—the entire journey from start to finish—is contained within the endless possibilities of the Fool.

What is inside the egg on which the Fool balances precariously? Everything and nothing at all. Every tarot card, and every outcome, in every possible combination — but also the endless void. All that is, all that isn't, all that may be, and all that never was.

Will the cosmic egg hatch? Will it shatter? Will it disappear forever, never to return? The human mind is not able to grasp such answers, even as there is a transcendent part of us that knows every sacred and abiding truth. So, the Fool does not spend time wondering or worrying. Instead, they choose to flow with what is happening, enjoy the journey, and boldly proceed. This is their secret key to accessing unlimited luck.

The Fool's etheric butterfly wings symbolize their budding transformation. This transformation is likely to arrive in ways both conventional (the upper wings) and unexpected (the lower, inverted wings). The wings are beset by symbols for the three alchemical elements that produce change and possess endless potential for congealing into physical form: sulfur, mercury, and salt.

The Fool is removing the obstruction from their eyes, for in their blind stumbling, they are beginning to see.

MEANINGS AND MESSAGES OF THE FOOL:

- Dive in with your whole self and flow with what's happening.
- Let yourself learn as you go.
- A portal of possibility is open: step through it.
- Be proactive and move forward without delay.
- Access luck by being fearless and bold.
- Admit you don't know and can't understand.
- There is great magic in stepping into the unknown.

- Surrender to uncertainty. More will be revealed when you proceed.
- Be down for the adventure.
- Be willing to make mistakes, for you will find immense value in those mistakes.

MEANINGS AND MESSAGES OF THE FOOL — REVERSED:

- You are blocking your progress by overthinking.
- Perfectionism is holding you back.
- You are refusing to see the positive potential that is right before your eyes.
- You will let this opportunity pass you by if you continue to delay.
- Banish over-caution and refuse to stay mired in your fear.
- Stop trying to see every step of the journey before you begin.
- Unblock yourself by reframing paralyzing fear as glorious excitement.
- See yourself as a student of life rather than believing you need to be a master.
- If you continue to play it safe, you will continue to be bored.
- The only way to guarantee you will never succeed is if you never try.

1. THE MAGICIAN

CREATE THE WORLD

GUIDANCE

This is a profound and pivotal moment. Do not sit idly by. Play a part in your own destiny and create your world according to your will.

You know what you want, and you have all the elements you need to fulfill your vision. Now, you must act.

The universal energies are available to you. Channel them wisely and with mastery. Be bold, crafty, and clever. Conjure up some magic and trust that your irresistible power, vision, and determination will carry you through.

Do not minimize or backpedal on your dreams. Be brazen and audacious in your wanting, and reach for all of it. You are ready. Proactively, daringly, meticulously bring your inner vision into outer manifestation.

DYNAMICS

The Magician is a lightning rod: he invites in and consciously embodies the electric power of pure potentiality and limitless light. He then focuses this power and channels it toward outcomes and conditions of his choosing. He knows he is not a bit player or a pawn, but a mighty sorcerer with the power to shape his destiny and command his world.

The Magician is not ashamed or afraid of his wishes, for he knows that acting on his heart's authentic desires will form a vital strand in the grand tapestry of light that interweaves and comprises all of existence in all directions of time.

His mouth is big because he is voracious: he wants to eat the world. Even his ravenous appetite is something he embraces, for it motivates him to continue seeking and finding victory, wonder, and delight.

While he knows that there is much that is out of his hands—such as the winds of change and the whims of chance—he also knows that even uncertainty can be leveraged to his benefit, so he happily rolls the dice with a valiant willingness to work with whatever may transpire.

SECRETS

Within the Magician's orbit are symbols for the three alchemical elements (salt, sulfur, and mercury) as well as symbols of the four elements of nature: earth, air, water, and fire. He is an active co-creator of his experience: a chemist combining the universal compounds to bring his cherished inner vision into form.

He rolls the dice with the unwavering belief that fate and chance are on his side. He knows that he cannot choose the numbers the dice come up with, but he can choose the story he tells himself about them, and the story is where the power lies.

He juggles because he is a master, and enjoys being in a flow state. When he synchronizes his mind with his body, it helps him stay awake and alert, so he can be in rhythm with divine orchestration and make the most of opportunities when they arise.

On his wand is a serpent coiled around an egg. What will hatch is unknown, and yet it is joyfully anticipated, and the Magician is ready for it. The serpent and egg incubate an exciting new world.

Above the Magician is the symbol for the planet Mercury, for the Magician is synonymous with Hermes/Mercury: the divine trickster, archetypal magician, master of technology and commerce, and winged messenger of the gods.

MEANINGS AND MESSAGES OF THE MAGICIAN:

- Be bold. Act swiftly and decisively on your desires and dreams.
- Invoke divine power and trust that you know what to do.
- You have the power to establish the conditions you desire, but you must proactively claim that power.
- Let confidence steer you forward into action.
- Create the space in your schedule and in the physical world for what you want to accomplish and experience.
- Work with spiritual principles to manifest your goals, while simultaneously taking concrete steps in the physical world.
- Set clear intentions and use them as a roadmap for action.
- You have enlisted the help of a wise doctor, counselor, or healer.

- Perform a ritual or spell to declare your intentions and attune to their frequency.

MEANINGS AND MESSAGES OF THE MAGICIAN — REVERSED:

- Stop waiting around for something to happen or for someone else to act. Your destiny is yours to create.
- Remember to ask the Divine for help.
- Reclaim your sense of personal power and move forward with the clear expectation that you are innately poised to succeed.
- Release stagnation, procrastination, and negative self-talk.
- Your actions (or non-actions) are not in alignment with your desires, but this is an easy fix. Simply shift your habits to support your goals.
- Don't just act, and don't just ask the Divine for help. You must do both, in tandem, if you want to succeed.
- Even if you think you already know what you want, it will benefit you to clearly formulate and write out your intentions. Phrase them in the present tense, as if they are already true.
- Carefully review and revisit information you've received from a doctor, counselor, or healer; wait until you've consulted with such a person before you proceed.
- Don't discount the power of magical and spiritual work, such as rituals, spells, affirmations, and visualizations.

2. THE HIGH PRIESTESS

MYSTIC SILENCE

GUIDANCE

Be silent and still, relaxed and yet utterly awake. Let go of your human ego and open to infinity. Connect with your nonverbal inner knowing without feeling the need to immediately act or logically understand.

Cultivate equilibrium. First, release the need to dazzle or impress. Next, remove your attention from the surface appearance of things and gaze into existence's timeless and inscrutable depths. Look beyond the fleeting carnival rides and fireworks and place your awareness on the primordial nighttime sea.

Your consciousness is everywhere, and who you are is eternal. You temporarily seem to appear as a tiny little self-contained creature on the surface of the earth, but in fact you are boundless, timeless, and immortal: interconnected with everything.

The High Priestess holds all secrets and mysteries, and points you toward the mystical, the wordless, and the vast.

DYNAMICS

Without the High Priestess' silence, we miss out on life's depth. We live on the surface of things, wondering why we play without feeling amused and consume without feeling fulfilled. We look for guidance to come to light in the form of words and actions, when it is waiting for us there in the darkness, beyond logic, outside of language, and independent of what we can perceive through our five senses alone.

Dazzled and distracted, we burn ourselves out, and we leave no room for the magic to flow in. We think we need to build a suave persona and amass an extraordinary fortune, when who we are and what we have are already vastly more valuable than what we can quantify or see.

The High Priestess asks you to cultivate a new kind of mastery: not one where you are actively the boss of things, but passively, naturally, one with everything. You flow where the river flows: downward, on the path of least resistance, and toward the sea. Like sea glass, your harsh edges are smoothed away.

You can help this along through meditation, conscious breathing, soaking in a bath, stargazing, walking slowly in nature, or spending time near a natural body of water.

SECRETS

The High Priestess embodies the alchemical dissolution process, when the ash of our egoic pretenses is dissolved and washed away in water, and we let go of the myths and masks that keep us separate and small.

For you are not your face, or your name, or your markers of human status, or even your personality traits. You are Infinity, momentarily playing within the illusion of form. A sparkle of sunlight on a wave, or a raindrop on its way back to the ocean — ever-so-briefly holding the shape of something separate, but not intrinsically or essentially separate at all.

In addition to being aligned with the water element and the moon, the High Priestess is the alchemical White Queen — the passive principle that corresponds with the element of mercury. Alchemical lore marries her to the Hierophant, the Red King, who holds the energy of the element of sulfur. This marriage of the passive to the active is the magic combination that instigates, informs, and defines the alchemist's creations.

She is between the worlds and the polarities. She is neutral and impartial, poised without self-consciousness, form and spirit in dynamic balance.

MEANINGS AND MESSAGES OF THE HIGH PRIESTESS:

- Take a step back, relax, and quiet your mind.
- Once you are steeped in silence and calm, consult your abiding inner knowing.
- First, let go of worry and frenetic thought. Then, practice intuitive and mystical arts.
- Meditate regularly.
- Contemplate the unknowable mysteries.
- You are a priestess or priest: do not see this as a self-aggrandizing title or role, but as a calling to dissolve your

ego, get comfortable with the mystery, and hold the space for magic to occur.
- Embrace the mystery and surrender to the flow of life.
- Align with silence and space, and your inspiration will be renewed.

MEANINGS AND MESSAGES OF THE HIGH PRIESTESS — REVERSED:

- If you continue to deal with a problem in the same way, you will continue to fail. Stop fighting what is happening and take a break so you can realign with universal energies.
- Your intuition has been obscured. Release inner worry and outer drama to uncover it.
- You are more agitated than you realize. Reestablish equilibrium by going on a retreat, soaking in a bath, or otherwise taking some quiet time alone without technology.
- Begin a daily meditation habit or get an existing one back on track.
- Stop fearing the unknown. Instead, let it propel you forward into adventure and calculated risk.
- Release the need to impress and let go of any performative aspects of your spirituality.
- Release the need for logical understanding and the desire to act constantly.
- Clear any unnecessary clutter and cancel gratuitous commitments to create the space and time for relaxation, inspiration, and spiritual work.

3. THE EMPRESS
GODDESS ON EARTH

GUIDANCE

Abundant prosperity is coming through you and to you. Revel in your senses, luxuriate in the gifts of the physical world, and give birth to beauty. Be proud of your feminine energy and embody the Goddess on Earth.

The Empress is a positive omen: a loving mother who provides wealth, pleasure, fertility, and luck. Relax your body, connect with the earth, and receive. Don't actively chase relationships or conditions. Instead, settle into your throne and naturally attract all that you desire. Be the Empress. Regally lift your hand, lovingly speak your intentions, and effortlessly draw it all in.

Just as there are times to toil and strive, there are times to taste the sweetness of the harvest and happily savor all you've earned. Now is a time to appreciate, and to call in even more blessings by simply being your lush and elegant self.

DYNAMICS

The Empress is womanly fullness and the luminous sensuality of summer: a red poppy, a verdant meadow, and a field of ripe, golden wheat, undulating in the gentle summer breeze. She holds a divine child in her womb and sings mellifluously of the glories of femininity. She smells of flowers and soil, and she radiates the wisdom of Gaia: our loving, receptive, and generous Mother Earth.

Just as a seed, a sprout, a flower, and an entire field of flowers stay in one place while growing, flourishing, and offering their profound beauty to the world, you need not rush around to experience all the magic that is already within you.

As you open your senses to present-moment enjoyment, you will attract even more to enjoy.

SECRETS

The Empress is veiled, for in addition to being contained within her body, her divine beauty is non-local: it is everywhere and in everything. It is the multifaceted, variegated magic of the entire manifest world. It is the wordless mystery that gives birth to beauty. Beneath the veil, she sits on a throne of red jasper and wears a round crown of stars: plugged into the iron-rich ore of the soil and channeling all the wisdom of the infinite light.

She is the Goddess as Mother, the White Queen (mercury and the lunar principle), who is wed to the Red King (sulfur and the solar principle) in the alchemical union that gives birth to creation and allows us to bring our deep desires and conscious wishes into form.

Within her womb are the universal substance and the alchemical elements in their most fertile aspect. This is where the pure potential of the Fool coalesces and takes on a tangible form.

MEANINGS AND MESSAGES OF THE EMPRESS:

- Abundance and wealth are on the horizon for you: enjoy them.
- Embody your femininity and take joy in your beauty.
- You are in a fertile period: preparing to give birth to a baby, a project, or a beautiful new condition.
- Celebrate the fruits of your efforts and calmly wield your Empress-like grace.
- Express your authority without struggling, striving, or forcing.
- Be proud of your body, just as it is.
- Eat plenty of wholesome, delicious food and savor life's sensual pleasures.
- Call or spend time with your mom or a maternal figure in your life.
- Call on the Great Goddess, and allow yourself to be nurtured, treasured, and soothed.
- Expect wonderful things: boons and blessings of all varieties are certainly on their way.

MEANINGS AND MESSAGES OF THE EMPRESS — REVERSED:

- To make way for abundance and wealth, stop and celebrate all the blessings you already have.
- Don't be ashamed of your femininity. Take time for self-care. Lovingly attend to your style and beauty.
- Don't be impatient with what you're bringing forth: honor the creative birthing process by relaxing and giving yourself the nourishment you need.
- Don't berate yourself or force yourself to work ceaselessly. Take time off to notice and congratulate yourself for all that you've already created and manifested.
- You will be more effective when you act from calm relaxation rather than ego-centered striving.
- Take steps to heal your body image.
- Heal your relationship with food and take the time to gather and prepare healthy and delicious meals.
- Heal old wounds and patterns related to your mother or a maternal figure.
- Release feelings of unworthiness and open up to the endless gifts of nourishment the Great Goddess yearns to provide.
- Change your inner monologue to one of joyful expectation. Instead of worrying, know that you are a treasured divine child, and allow yourself to receive an endless flow of wealth and privilege.

4. THE EMPEROR
DISCIPLINE BY DESIGN

GUIDANCE

Find or assemble a set of rules you respect, then follow them. Impose your will through wise and decisive leadership. Dismiss pleas for unearned leniency, refuse to be persuaded by emotional appeals, and impartially lay down the law.

There are times when bending or ignoring the rules will serve you well, but this is not one of those times. It's true that the persistent tyranny of the patriarchy has motivated many of us to reject anything that resembles stern discipline and rigid structure. But this does not always serve us; individually and as a culture, we require well-defined, clearly enforced laws, habits, and guidelines if we want to thrive.

Even in the creative, fluid realms of art and spirituality, without a regular, daily (or almost daily) practice, we will fail to achieve our goals. Similarly, commitment to a romantic relationship demands clearly defined rules and boundaries. The Emperor's structure provides a solid container in which we can lovingly hold the effervescent elixir of our inspiration, pleasure, and love.

DYNAMICS

Wise leadership demands a precise balance. Totalitarianism doesn't allow space for collaboration and new ideas, but anarchy prevents organization and constructive forward movement. The highest potential of the Emperor is the midpoint between the two: a strong leader who encourages his subjects to be more, not less, of themselves, both individually and as a collective.

In our personal lives, the Emperor represents our motivation and ability to form positive habits and create the space for our cherished goals to manifest into form. For example, you may say you want to paint, you may buy the art supplies, and you may even sit down in front of the canvas with your brushes every now and again. But if you don't carve out regular intervals of prescribed time to practice your craft—say, one hour, three or five or seven days a week, whether or not you're "in the mood"—you will remain a dilettante and dabbler, wishing idly for something that all along is within your own power to obtain.

Or you may be a member of a group with no clear leader. Perhaps everyone in the group wants the same thing, but no one trusts their authority enough to give the group the direction and discipline it needs to succeed. This is a group in need of the Emperor's wisdom. The Emperor prioritizes forward movement and collective success over his personal desire to be comfortable or liked. While he may seem callous, he's never unfair, and he's willing to alienate some people, push himself out of his comfort zone, and step on a few toes for the sake of advancing his cause.

SECRETS

Infinity pours into and out of the Emperor's throat as his decrees transcend his limited human ego to impose divine structure upon all he surveys. The butterfly symbolizes the Emperor's authority not just over life, but also over death and rebirth. The Emperor is the air element: thought, intellect, and ideas. The symbols for the alchemical elements come into various forms according to his firm declarations of what he will and won't allow.

He is veiled in red because he is aligned with the solar principle and the active alchemical element of sulfur. We see the hand of the Empress, the White Queen, who weds the Emperor, the Red King, in the alchemical marriage of mercury and sulfur, moon and sun, that gives form and aliveness to the alchemist's intentions.

Like the lead in a cosmic ballroom dance, the Emperor chooses the steps and holds the form for the Empress to twirl and unfurl. This is how the divine beauty and creative abundance of nature expresses itself within the shared bounds and agreements of human culture.

Beneath the red veil, the Emperor wears armor, for his role requires stoicism and impartiality.

MEANINGS AND MESSAGES OF THE EMPEROR:

- Establish and stick to a set of daily habits that support your goals.

- Take the lead at work or in some sort of coalition or group.
- Make rules or follow rules.
- Fashion your physical world in a way that will support and fuel your intentions: for example, create a workspace for your art or business, and gather the tools and ingredients you need.
- Call or spend time with your dad or a paternal figure in your life.
- Choose your direction based on logic rather than emotion.
- Prioritize personal and collective success.

MEANINGS AND MESSAGES OF THE EMPEROR — REVERSED:

- Bust out of a rut by making the clear decision to establish the habits that will support your goals.
- Stop resisting the call to lead.
- Stop breaking or ignoring the rules.
- Clear physical clutter and reclaim your physical space so you can finally get to work in an efficient and effective way.
- Take steps to heal old wounds and patterns related to your dad or a paternal figure.
- Stop letting your emotions get in the way of doing what you need to do.
- You may need to make an unpopular choice or get into a habit that is challenging or uncomfortable to establish.

5. THE HIEROPHANT

5 . THE HIEROPHANT

SPIRITUAL LAW

GUIDANCE

There is great value in learning and working with the mystical secrets of the ages. There are countless spiritual paths, but ideally, they all lead to universal oneness and love. Seek out the teachings that speak to you and commit to putting them into practice.

Study the spiritual cosmologies and technologies that interest and transfix you. Learn from teachers, but don't hand your power over to any of them. Read books, but don't consider any book to be intrinsically holy or literally true.

Teachers are people and books are written by people, and the best people can do is point the way. No human can possibly be the sole transmitter of truth. Still, transcendent truths often shine through words and forms. This is why we can learn from elders and those who have come before.

Diligently search for spiritual truth in the precepts, rituals, and stories of various traditions, from the ancient mystery schools to the modern and conventional creeds. If you're not sure where to begin, let your inspiration be your motivation and your guide. Research what interests you. Experiment and find out what works. Assemble a set of practices and construct a body of wisdom that resonates with you and serves you well.

DYNAMICS

While our spiritually inclined ancestors usually did not have much of a choice regarding what spiritual iteration they would pursue, we now have access to vast information about the sacred traditions of every continent and culture, from ancient times to the present day.

In some ways, this makes for a more complex and confusing path, but it ultimately blesses us with the precious personal agency that has historically been withheld by those in power. We now hold the keys to our own enlightenment. We need not bow to humans who declare, exploit, and monetize their supposed spiritual authority. We need not swear allegiance to a congregation or unquestioningly conform to a dogma. We can contemplate the Great Mystery independently, personally decide what feels right to us (and what doesn't), and tap into guidance in our own time and way.

The Hierophant counsels you to establish spiritual order in your own inner landscape. Create an altar or ritual space in your home. Invoke the Divine every day in a way that feels powerful to you and ask for the guidance and support you need. Find a meditation practice that works for you and enforce it daily. Awaken a sense of wonderment. Cultivate awe. Work with Spirit to manifest your desires. Establish peace within. Be an emissary of love and a guiding light of positive change.

SECRETS

The Hierophant is the High Priestess' partner. He is the Red King (embodiment of sulfur, the sun, and the active principle) who marries the White Queen (embodiment of mercury, the moon, and the passive principle).

If the High Priestess is the watery womb of night, the Hierophant is the fiery seed of day. By providing spiritual stories and practices accessible to humans, the Hierophant helps us harness the vastness of Infinity, giving us language for the wordless, and some small bit of mastery over that which is beyond our ability to grasp.

The Hierophant is the fertile spark of spiritual wisdom contained within sacred texts and alchemical treatises. He is the flash that spawns our powerful connection to the Divine.

MEANINGS AND MESSAGES OF THE HIEROPHANT:

- Study and practice spiritual practices and traditions that interest you.
- Find inspiration in the wisdom of the ages.
- Work with a therapist or counselor.
- Establish habits that support your spiritual unfolding, such as meditation, divination, and ritual.
- Assemble your own book of shadows: a collection of your cherished spiritual practices, rituals, and beliefs.
- Trust your own intrinsic connection to the Divine.
- Step into a role as a spiritual leader, teacher, healer, or guide.

MEANINGS AND MESSAGES OF THE HIEROPHANT — REVERSED:

- Don't feel limited by one spiritual practice or path: if you feel stuck or bored, it's probably time to branch out.
- Don't cling to dogma. Be open-minded and fluid as you seek out transcendent and universal truths.
- Even though speaking to a therapist or counselor can feel vulnerable, transcend your reluctance and reach out for help.
- Don't be a dabbler: just because you're forging your own path doesn't mean you shouldn't fully commit to that path by practicing it daily.
- But don't be overly rigid either: it's okay to change your mind and switch up your spiritual self-expression.
- Be wary of cult-like dynamics or high-control groups: take steps to extricate yourself if you discover someone is controlling you.
- Release fear about being a spiritual teacher or leader.

6. THE LOVERS
DIVINE UNION

GUIDANCE

A partnership is becoming more than the sum of its parts. A powerful connection is brewing. Make a clear choice to stimulate new conditions and help move things forward in a positive way.

A magical union is of the essence now.

If this is a romantic relationship, this person may be a life partner. But no matter how long your energies mingle and your paths intertwine, you will each play a vital and transformational role in the other's life.

If this is a friendship or business partnership, you have much to share with each other and learn.

This is always a message about making a choice, for every choice contains two polarized ingredients: a yes and a no. By choosing one path over another, you actualize one avenue while refusing the others. The yes and no combine within the cauldron of your decision to form an effervescent brew of constructive change.

In all cases, let love guide and illuminate. Love clarifies and catalyzes.

DYNAMICS

In divine union, the Lovers combine their energies to create something new. Just as procreation is the alchemy of fertilization and gestation, all creation is a complex interplay and intermingling of dark and light, passive and active, night and day. The alchemist chooses to be a conscious co-creator of this cosmic brew by swirling their actions and intentions into the mix.

In embracing commitment, you boldly embark on one trajectory, to the exclusion of all other potential avenues. While this can feel like a loss of possibility, without making a choice, you go nowhere, so no possibilities are actualized at all. What, here, is your yes? If you don't choose, you will remain stuck. So don't hesitate. Step into the cauldron of relationship, say a decisive goodbye to all other avenues and potential avenues, and say hello to the exciting and transformational qualities of your yes.

SECRETS

Independence, in our culture, is fetishized and overrated. We all have hungry souls because we all need connection and support, and we all want a hand to hold as we move through the blessings and challenges of this mysterious life. This is not because we're needy, but because we are social creatures who thrive on collaboration, with hearts that long to cherish and be cherished, love and be loved.

We are wired to connect, and for various reasons, we all have default ways of connecting. If you fear connection and push people away, you may have an avoidant attachment style. If you constantly worry that you have said or done something wrong, or that friends, family members, or partners will disappear or stop loving you, you may have an anxious attachment style. If any of this rings true, you will benefit by cultivating what is called a secure attachment style. Having a secure attachment style—trusting others and feeling comfortable in your ability to work out any challenges that may come your way—is the single most powerful factor when it comes to relationship security and satisfaction, which in turn will support you in every other area of your life.

The symbols on the cauldron communicate the harmonious mixture of two souls and the consequent healing of their various approaches to love. When we feel supported and safe in our primary relationships, we become emboldened to take risks and try new things. In turn, we manifest new and greater levels of happiness, freedom, and success.

MEANINGS AND MESSAGES OF THE LOVERS:

- Let love guide you as you make a clear choice and act on it.
- A vital and mutually beneficial romantic relationship, partnership, or friendship is present or is about to appear.
- A love relationship has the potential to heal you and bless your life in countless ways.

- A business partnership will bring forth positive new conditions.
- This is not a passing fling, but rather a soulmate bond.
- A relationship with another will enhance your life and augment your power. Together, you become more than the sum of your parts.

MEANINGS AND MESSAGES OF THE LOVERS — REVERSED:

- Procrastinating about a choice will keep you stuck.
- You are pushing someone away through avoidance or anxiety: cultivate a secure attachment style and open your heart to love.
- You are placing too much stock in independence. Remember that we all need help, support, connection, and affection to thrive.
- Air out any concerns about a business partnership or potential business partnership so you can cooperatively heal and get back on track.
- Don't keep pouring out the cauldron before the magic has a chance to brew. Stick around long enough to allow the potion of your relationship to steep, swirl, and coagulate.
- In some cases, it may be time to be grateful for what you have shared, and then to let go and move on. Don't try to manipulate another or force an outcome that is outside your control.

7. THE CHARIOT

SELF-MASTERY

GUIDANCE

Harness and integrate the various aspects of your psyche. Bring your unconscious desires into the light of awareness to harmoniously blend them with your conscious efforts. Be the most effective and empowered version of yourself so you can steer your life according to your will.

Let your curiosity about yourself propel you into your next stage of personal authority and power. What drives you? What secrets have you been keeping from yourself? What do you truly desire, and what do you secretly fear? What thoughts and feelings have you been renouncing, denying, and pushing away? Whom do you worry you are, and whom do you most wish to be? When you invite all parts of you to be present, and you direct them to work as one diverse but coordinated group, you will be ready for the journey, and perfectly poised to navigate yourself in the direction of your choosing.

In alchemy, this is sublimation, or the lifelong process of personal development. Psychologically speaking, this is a form of individuation: distinguishing yourself from your family, community, and culture while shedding more and more light on the inner workings of your mind and emotions, so your personality can become more resonant, and you can employ greater mastery over yourself and your world.

DYNAMICS

You are born from the prima materia, which includes genes, atoms, electrons, and stardust: the primary physical elements. The prima materia—the chaotic and disparate brew of materials that congealed to form you—also contains the etheric and energetic qualities of your culture, community, and the beliefs and events that contributed to the existence of your ancestors, that were present for your parents, and that were swirling around at the time of your conception.

Although your birth was, in itself, a differentiation from the prima materia, as an alchemist or a spiritual seeker, you are now being called to proactively distinguish your individuality even more. Instead of being a submissive follower or an indistinct member of the crowd, mindlessly stumbling through life without agency or a clear sense of purpose, you gaze bravely into your depths, learn who you are, decide what you care about, and choose the steps that move you toward your goals.

SECRETS

The glorious sun is the opus: the great work of the alchemist, magician, and seeker. This is a lifelong process of learning about yourself, healing from your past, and transforming your challenges into fuel for your journey toward ever-expanding levels of happiness, authority, wisdom, and success.

Along with the symbols of the alchemical elements, here we see the symbol for sublimation: the personal development that brings the unconscious into the realm of the conscious and sheds clarifying light on the innermost workings of the soul. Through integration, individuation, and sublimation, you bring your unique destiny out of the formless by giving it form. With your feet planted firmly on the earth, you harness the elements, anchor your visions, and gather the sustained focus and drive you need for the triumphant adventure ahead.

MEANINGS AND MESSAGES OF THE CHARIOT:

- You have everything you need to succeed. Employ all aspects of yourself and take concrete action steps toward your goal.
- Harness your inner resources to overcome inertia and manifest your desires.
- Admit, embrace, and be proud of every aspect of yourself, and let this pride inspire you to be who you are and do what you want to do.
- Acknowledge conflicting feelings and traits within you, but notice the value they all have to offer, and consciously interweave them to craft a vehicle of wholeness and power.
- Notice how far you've come in your spiritual path and inner work. Employ the mastery you've gained to move forward with confidence and courage.
- Your life is yours to lead, so take the reins without apology or delay.

MEANINGS AND MESSAGES OF THE CHARIOT — REVERSED:

- Stop procrastinating. Don't give away your power or question your ability to succeed.
- Bust out of a rut by getting clear on what you want and honest about how you feel. Then, make a concrete plan for manifesting your goals and take action on it.
- Don't fear who you are or deny what you want. Be brave. Commit to integrating all aspects of yourself.
- Your own complexity is paralyzing you: just because you have complicated and conflicted feelings about something, don't let that prohibit you from acting.
- Your fear has been holding you back from your spiritual and personal development work. Make the conscious choice to transcend that fear so you can claim your authority and wield your power.
- Stop living by default or handing off your decisions to others. While it's often helpful to ask for and receive support from others, you must choose your own path and forge your own way.

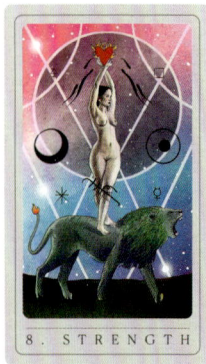

8. STRENGTH

SELF-MASTERY

GUIDANCE

This is a time of gentle yet comprehensive triumph. You are strong, capable, and wise. As you wield your confidence, the universe and universal energies consistently support your success.

Relax, let go of worry, and allow divine strength to flow through you. Benefit from all the life lessons you've already gained and all the diligent self-improvement work you have already put in. If you consult your inner wisdom and reflect on your past experiences and insights, you will know you are more than qualified to handle whatever comes your way.

Poise, ease, and relentlessly positive expectation will serve you well. This is the power that comes from mildness and the self-assurance that comes from humility.

There is magic in the active equilibrium between relaxation and action, independence and collaboration, structure and flow. Dynamic balance appears still, but requires awake aliveness in every muscle, atom, and focused thought.

DYNAMICS

The sun is unimaginably strong, and yet it can caress our skin like the tenderest kiss. The moon is an inert sphere of receptive rock, yet it manages the seas, shines light in the darkness, and keeps the spin of the very planet in balance. Similarly, you can relax as you hold your fiery heart high, perched effortlessly atop the fierce lion that you alone have tamed. Authentic power is wielded with an abundance of ease.

This enduring quality of strength is presently available to you. Summon it and attune to it. Find your graceful and dignified composure and let it shine softly from your heart like a swirling cauldron of both sun and moon. This radiant light will illuminate your way.

SECRETS

Sun and moon represent the living balance of masculine and feminine energies: day and night, active and passive, potential and actualized.

Also present are the alchemical symbols for volatile—or changeable—alchemical ingredients in perfect symmetry and balance. This is the formula for an awakened poise within the personality and soul. The *prima materia* of the psyche is distilled and then masterfully combined to ferment into a golden, glowing potion of inner awakening and outer success.

The green lion is the sun's power made manifest as the verdant and nourishing earth. The contained spark of the sun's fierce fire burns brightly at the end of the lion's tail and the woman's flaming heart.

The lion roars as he devotedly carries his human friend upon his back. The woman's posture is both tranquil and vigorously awake. Great power has been harnessed in this partnership, and it is to the mutual benefit of both players, as well as everyone who observes them and is drawn into their sphere.

MEANINGS AND MESSAGES OF STRENGTH:

- Realize how strong you are.
- Relax and allow your strength and mastery to shine through.
- You have gathered the wisdom and self-mastery you need to easily triumph and succeed.
- You have every reason to be confident.
- Wield your mastery with ease.
- Be both gentle and strong.
- Lead with both firmness and understanding.
- Infinite wisdom and power are available to you. Ask for divine support and allow it to flow in.
- In taking full responsibility, you will find ease.

MEANINGS AND MESSAGES OF STRENGTH — REVERSED:

- Summon your courage to turn this situation around.
- You don't need to fake it. You have access to authentic power if you will only allow yourself to believe it.
- Recognize how far you've come and how much you've already conquered; you will summon the confidence to face whatever may arise.
- Change your default from anxiety and fear to confidence and calm, and clearly set boundaries as needed.
- Acknowledge the things you are good at, and stop hiding your light from yourself and the world.
- Don't seek to intimidate, belittle, bully, or falsely impress. True self-confidence does not force itself on others. It shines gently, but consistently, like the crescent moon and early springtime sun.
- Anxiety about your self-worth is causing you to act ineffectively, but this need not continue.
- Stop pushing away divine favor and earthly support. Relax, breathe, ask for help, and allow yourself to receive that help now.
- Blaming others perpetually will keep you stuck. Even if the problem isn't your fault, take responsibility for it, find the blessing in it, and make it work for you.

9. THE HERMIT

WISDOM IN SILENCE

G U I D A N C E

Meditate, pray, and immerse yourself in the healing magic of silence. Retreat from the world and go within. Consult the immeasurable wisdom that is the essence of your very self.

Don't rush into the next thing. Even if you have the impulse or craving to know precisely what subsequent step to take in the physical world, make friends with ambiguity and surrender to the not-knowing. Time and space will provide you with the perspective and guidance you need.

Wisdom does not always coincide with certainty, and insight at times requires that you surrender the need to understand. The ego wants to see the whole, linear path from beginning to end. All the while, the eternal soul is one with infinity's unfathomable amniotic brew.

Whether you retreat for an hour, a day, a weekend, a week, or even more, solitary alone time is imperative. Withdraw from or severely limit conversation, technology, and social interactions so you can listen to silence and, eventually, hear the clear and loving inner guidance of your soul.

DYNAMICS

The Hermit keeps his dwelling neat by sweeping, dusting, and organizing his sparse belongings. He sits for hours in silence, listening to and aligning with that which is beyond words.

He lets the conflicting inner voices and components separate, dissolve, and settle like stars after the big bang and pebbles at the bottom of a stream. No matter how long it takes, he waits patiently until the clouds have dispersed, the various elements have distinguished themselves, and the water runs clear.

It is impossible to rush, manipulate, or pressure him. Supremely grounded and immaculately aligned with the open sky, he sits calmly at the top of his mountain. He is perfectly at peace with the mystery and all that cannot be known, so he answers to no one. He keeps his own counsel and communes solely with the conscious aliveness that lives in silence and space.

The Hermit has seen it all, not just once, but countless times, in various incarnations, throughout the millennia. He knows that time is a spiral rather than a line and that space stretches outward in all directions but still somehow doubles back on itself. Cycles do not disturb him, for they are ceaseless, and endings and beginnings are one and the same.

He is Merlin and Lao Tzu, the archetypal magician and sage. Dissolved into the waters of eternity, he is one with all wisdom: birthless, deathless, and outside the confines of time.

SECRETS

The lantern is clear inner knowing and the ability to see into the darkest depths. Within the eye socket, we peer into the cosmic and eternal nature of the Hermit's soul. The white beard is a symbol of patience and the wisdom of age. The sacred geometry and alchemical symbols illustrate the dissolution of the ego and the self, to reveal the *prima materia*: the primordial building blocks of nature, spirit, and the Divine.

MEANINGS AND MESSAGES OF THE HERMIT:

- Retreat into silence.
- A spiritual teacher or wise person has appeared in your life.
- Take your time and go within.
- Meditate and pray.
- With time and patience, the dust will settle, and you will know what to do.
- Live with order, simplicity, and cleanliness.
- Spend some quality time alone.
- Cultivate patience. Get comfortable with not knowing and not understanding. When the time is right, you will know how to proceed.
- The answers you seek are within.
- Even if you think you've taken enough time away, take a little bit more.

MEANINGS AND MESSAGES OF THE HERMIT — REVERSED:

- Reduce overwhelm and simplify your schedule.
- Don't put all your faith in a counselor, elder, or spiritual teacher. Consult your own wisdom as well.
- Don't rush around looking for answers outside of yourself.
- Cultivate a regular meditation habit and solitary spiritual practice.
- It is not wise to rush ahead. First, stop and reflect to establish equilibrium.
- Your home's disarray is blocking you from divine flow: clean, simplify, and organize.
- While it's important to spend time with friends and there are times when it's helpful to ask others' opinions, now is a time to take space and spend time alone.
- Don't think you need to know everything right now. Be patient and find the wisdom in uncertainty. When the time is right, direction and guidance will arise from your inner silence and space.
- Quiet your mind so you can sense the loving direction that comes from within.
- You've been cloistered long enough. A cycle has completed. Consolidate and integrate all you've gained and take steps to return to the world.

10. WHEEL OF FORTUNE

DESTINY INTERVENES

GUIDANCE

A significant change is coming, or you are already in the middle of one. This is a part of the big picture and plan. Let go of the past as you open to the future, and fortune will find you.

Every life has surprise turns. So, if there's one thing you can expect, it's that which you didn't expect. Or perhaps something you did expect, but not so soon or not in the form in which it happens to arise.

The Serenity Prayer says, "God[dess], grant me the serenity to accept the things I cannot change, the courage to change the things I can, and the wisdom to know the difference." Indeed, this is the philosophy that will serve you best when you spin the wheel of fate and show up at the roulette table of life.

Beautiful changes are on the horizon for you. This will require you to surrender and say goodbye to one or more treasured conditions or blessings from your past. Even the most wonderful new beginning comes with its share of inevitable endings. To experience today to the fullest, you must let go of yesterday.

Radical acceptance will help you flow with the changes with ease. Cultivate unconditional calm and let go of fear.

Even as the wheel turns, you will find stillness at the center. As you anticipate and move through this change, meditate, pray, smile, open your heart, and find peace within.

DYNAMICS

Alchemists know that change is the way of life, so they learn to work with it rather than against it. When you acknowledge that much is beyond your control, you'll discover that there is also much within your control, particularly in how you respond to what happens. Find a wordless and visceral resonance with the turning wheel. Ask Spirit for help and set the clear intention to synchronize yourself with divine orchestration. Even if it's a wild ride, the unfolding of your life's most ideal journey will ensue.

SECRETS

Observe the double ouroboros: two snakes, each eating the other's tail. This is a symbol of infinity, creation, volatility, and change. Two separate forces come together like day and night, the beginning of one devouring the end of the other in an endless dance, consuming and assimilating the old to formulate and nourish the new.

In the middle is the all-seeing eye: calm insight at the center of the swirling storm. There is a blindfold because the whole picture is not accessible to us while we are here, in temporary human form, playing the game of life. We can't know all, but our Divine Source does know all. Inwardly connecting with this Source will steady us, infuse us with luck, and prepare us for positive change.

Flanking the eye are the symbols for gold and silver, sun and moon. Above, we see a combined symbol of mercury and the sun above a grounded container of silver fumes. Below, we see the symbols for sulfur and salt. In each corner, the symbols of the four elements appear: earth, air, fire, and water. The *prima materia* is present in a volatile form, giving life to adventure, destiny, co-creation, and the alchemy of change.

MEANINGS AND MESSAGES OF WHEEL OF FORTUNE:

- Expect and prepare for a positive change.
- Flow with what happens while being ready to embrace opportunities when they arise.
- Prioritize excitement and adventure.
- Take a chance on your dreams.
- Unexpected events are aligning you with your destiny.
- Meditate, pray, and ask for divine and earthly support as you consciously align with your Source. This will steady you for the beautiful changes ahead and open you up to your good.
- There is an obvious or hidden blessing for you in the changes you are experiencing now.

MEANINGS AND MESSAGES OF WHEEL OF FORTUNE — REVERSED:

- Do your best to let go of fear and make friends with uncertainty.
- Surrender to the flow of change. Fighting it is a waste of your time and energy.
- Transform fear of uncertainty into excitement for what is to come.
- Even when changes are unstoppable, there are still some things that you can control. Take care of yourself, ask for support, and find calm within the center of the storm.
- Make peace with an ending of some kind. Grieve if you need to. Then let go. In releasing the old, you will open to the new.
- Support is here for you in both the divine and physical realms, but you must remember to ask for it and allow yourself to receive it.
- You are feeling overwhelmed by change, but if you can get grounded and connect with the Divine, you will find that even the most challenging events contain beautiful blessings and priceless opportunities.

11. JUSTICE
EQUALIZING FORCE

GUIDANCE

Divine regulation or human law is intervening to establish fairness for all concerned. If you have a choice to make, weigh your options and decide wisely. Impartially consider all the angles, viewpoints, and concerns.

Sometimes, life presents us with restrictions or challenges that support us in learning how to do better than we've done in the past. This isn't a rebuke, but a loving correction that can help us grow. By recognizing the lesson, you can offer gratitude, free yourself from limitations, and emerge stronger and wiser than you otherwise would have been.

Other times, we seek human justice or request divine justice because we have been wronged, or someone has taken advantage of a person, group, or situation we care about. If this is the case for you, this card should be a welcome sight, for you will find the restitution you seek.

Finally, this card urges you to decide carefully. Don't be hasty or irresponsible in your choice. Prioritize balance, harmony, and fairness. Patiently examine all possibilities and perspectives before you make your move.

DYNAMICS

While pure divine wisdom transcends judgment, punishment, and reward, in this human experience, we participate in the drama that is born from the illusion of separation. This is why we need justice: to curb unfairness by reprimanding those who have behaved poorly, protecting the disenfranchised, and compensating those who have been wronged.

While undifferentiated divine light is whole and without polarities, this human experience is finite and polarized. As we interact with others and the physical world, we experience ups, downs, spirals, swirls, and the full spectrum of experience and emotion.

Justice stands with her bare feet on the earth and channels all the power of heaven. Indeed, she connects heaven with earth by conducting the eternal diamond light of infinity into the finite physical world of form. In so doing, she facilitates structure and illuminates a roadmap that helps us find equilibrium even within the uncharted chaos of human life.

SECRETS

Crowning Justice is the symbol of vitriol, the corrosive agent of change. Like justice itself, vitriol may seem harsh, but when used properly, it can immediately provide the corrective measures that are required.

The swords provide a portal to clarity. They cut away illusion, subterfuge, and all that is irrelevant to the situation at hand. They also hold a blindfold over her eyes. This symbolizes her ability to see with her heart and soul without getting blinded by prejudice, cowed by authority, or dazzled by worldly status.

Below the left scale, we see the symbol for disposition, which is the alchemical term for weighing an element to determine just the right proportion before adding it to the mix. Below the scale on the right, we see a teardrop from the divine ocean, symbolizing compassion, empathy, and understanding. Within the dynamic balance of impartial measurement and merciful understanding, we find the formula for justice.

MEANINGS AND MESSAGES OF JUSTICE:

- Fairness will prevail.
- You will be victorious in a legal dispute.
- Divine justice is intervening to establish fairness for all concerned.
- Be patient, weigh your options, and choose wisely.
- Before you proceed, relax, clear your mind, and systematically consider all your options and the perspectives and needs of everyone concerned.
- Prioritize justice, fairness, and balance for everyone concerned, and you will succeed.
- Strike a balance between forgiving compassion and strict adherence to the law.

MEANINGS AND MESSAGES OF JUSTICE — REVERSED:

- Fairness is temporarily blocked. Accept this, and, if possible, take steps to remedy it.
- You may not experience the outcome you seek in a legal dispute. Be compassionate with yourself and don't give up. Call on Spirit and ask for human support. There may be other avenues to pursue.
- This situation is out of balance. Simply being aware of this is the first step to setting it right.
- A past choice may have put you in a bind. Now you must choose differently to change your situation for the better.
- Don't be hasty. Stop rushing around. Take a step back, clear your mind, and patiently look at all the angles to get this situation back on track.
- Expand your awareness to consider all the factions. You may be overly focused on your own needs to the exclusion of others, or it may be the other way around. Look for the best possible outcome for all concerned, including yourself.
- You are either being too lenient or too severe. Temper one quality with the other in just the right amount.

12. THE HANGED

SACRIFICE THE EGO

GUIDANCE

Stop believing in "shoulds" — what should have happened, how things should look, or how things should unfold. Release all attempts to control what you can't control. Offer up your whole self to the mystery and the purifying flame of change.

Life is presenting you with the alchemical fire of opportunity, but you will only experience its blessings if you let yourself be consumed by its flames. Open your heart to the sky, divest yourself of struggle, and allow over-identification with your ego to be utterly reduced to ash.

Even though you are infinite and one with everything, when you were born into this human experience, you chose to temporarily appear as finite and separate. The ego is a name for this illusion — the illusion that you are a distinct, self-sustaining, and transitory creature. The ego is not bad in and of itself, but it transcends its rightful place and creates unnecessary confusion when it disguises itself as you.

Remember who you really are. You are the infinite light and the formless void, temporarily playing and experimenting within the appearance of form. You can use your current situation to realign with this truth. This will provide healing recalibration and assist you in moving forward in the most successful of ways.

If you can sacrifice your ego and flow with what happens, a seeming obstacle or problem will dissolve, revealing its true nature as a most exquisite gift.

DYNAMICS

When we make choices based on untrue narratives and ego-driven desires, we suffer, and create problems out of nothing. We commit to conditions we don't authentically want or refuse to see the blessings directly in front of us simply because they don't conform to an imaginary persona and false sense of self.

Sometimes, the ego tells us we are insignificant, and other times, it tells us we are extra special and entitled. Either way, the story is bogus. You are worthy of wonderful things, and the light you shine is vital and unique. But even as your uniqueness sets you apart, it's also true that you are no more and no less beloved and precious to the Divine than everyone else.

Luckily, the law of divine alchemy is intervening, offering you the perfect opportunity to restore your true self-worth and your inherent connection with divine orchestration and flow. The secret is to willingly hand over and offer up your attachment to how you appear and how things will unfold.

Allow yourself to know nothing and to be nothing. In this way, you will open to everything. You will restore your access to infinity, magic, and pure potentiality.

SECRETS

This is the alchemical process of calcification: when matter is placed above a fire until it is reduced to white ash. Instead of hiding away from her shame, the Hanged has made it into a sacred offering, so it can be purified and transmuted in Divinity's all-consuming fire.

Then, what was once heavy and stuck becomes fluid and light — an elixir of incandescent gold, appearing as fountains, swirls, and eddies of the vital essence, nourishing and fertilizing the celestial sea.

The four-armed cross above the Hanged is the alchemical symbol for vinegar, which purifies. We also see symbols for the sun and moon (gold and silver) as well as the three most basic alchemical elements of salt, sulfur, and mercury.

The snake, which is already free of ego, has appeared to help with the alchemical process. The pyramid is the sacred fire that facilitates complete surrender and utter transformation into the light.

MEANINGS AND MESSAGES OF THE HANGED:

- Relax, let go, and trust.
- This challenging time is an alchemical process of positive transformation.
- The more you surrender to what is already happening, the better the outcome of this situation will be.

- You can't rush this situation, but you can help it along by saying yes to it and becoming awake to the many possible blessings it contains.
- You are going through a profound and positive change.
- Be willing to be nothing and have nothing, and you will open to everything.

MEANINGS AND MESSAGES OF THE HANGED — REVERSED:

- You are hanging on to something too tightly. First, loosen your grip, then let go.
- You are prolonging the challenge by fighting against it. Flow with it instead.
- Your luck is temporarily blocked because you are resisting divine orchestration by attempting to force your will.
- Unblock your forward progress by releasing the desire to conform or to appear a certain way in the eyes of the world.
- Surrender to the unknown. Be honest about what you can and can't control and be willing to let the universe surprise and delight you with that which you didn't expect.
- If something didn't work out the way you wanted it to, reframe it as a learning experience. Reflect, regroup, and prepare to try again.

13. DEATH
DECAY NOURISHES

GUIDANCE

A sweeping change requires you to utterly let go. There is great power in this cataclysm. Dance exuberantly with death and make way for something beautiful and new.

It may surprise you to learn that most often, the Death card indicates an extreme yet positive change. Consider that even the most favorable new development forces you to say goodbye forever to a familiar—and likely comfortable or comforting—condition, such as a career, relationship status, or living situation.

When folks say they desire something, they don't often consider the stress and discomfort that will be associated with getting it. For example, while you will certainly cherish and delight in the experience of meeting a life partner, you will never again be able to return to the time before. Your life as a single person may not have been perfect, but it was what you knew, and it is destined to die before you can move forward into a beautiful new season of life.

Moving to a new city, too, asks us not only to embrace where we are going, but also to forsake where we have been. While there may be a day when we return for a visit or to stay, it will never be entirely the same.

Look deeply and you will know what you are sending off, even as you happily anticipate and sense what you are welcoming in.

D Y N A M I C S

Death's fire purifies and illuminates, while death's decay lends nourishment to the soil, allowing the fields to be fertile and the flowers to bloom. We can fear change all we want, but in courageously embracing it and dancing with it, we open to more possibilities and a more expansive capacity for joy. This is pure alchemy — the alchemical process in its most essential form.

Fear of death, fear of upheaval, and fear of the image on this very card all indicate a wonderful opportunity to unlock your power and clear the way to your life's most ideal unfolding. Breathe deeply into the fear until you feel it move and incrementally translate into exhilarating excitement for what is to come. This is like fanning the flames on a funeral pyre, transforming what is dead, decaying, and inert into bright light and precious fuel.

S E C R E T S

Death arrives on a yellow horse branded with the alchemical symbol for rot. Death floats gracefully, wielding the sparkling stars of rebirth and devastating change. His shadowy gaze obliterates, purifies, and transmutes, destroying what has been to make way for all the beautiful blessings that shall be.

Look closely in the background and you will see a boat on the horizon. It is ready to carry you forward, away from all you have known, directly into the thrilling rebirth that awaits.

Even when you return to this very river of life, death, and rebirth, the river itself will never be the same.

MEANINGS AND MESSAGES OF DEATH:

- A positive change requires you to let go of something forever.
- A new phase begins as an old phase passes away.
- A birth or rebirth is about to carry you away from all you have known.
- Mourn and grieve as appropriate, but also celebrate the fires of death as they purify the old to make room for the new.
- Notice what is rotting so you can make it into fertilizer and use it to plant a new crop.
- Surrender to this period of emotional pain or chaotic transformation, knowing that it will ultimately lead you in the direction of your destiny.
- You are clearing the way for positive change by ending an unhealthy relationship or letting go of clutter in your home or workspace.
- You have reason to celebrate. A vast and exhilarating change is at hand.

MEANINGS AND MESSAGES OF DEATH — REVERSED:

- You are holding on to something that is not what it once was. Acknowledge this and let it go.
- A new phase is coming whether you're ready for it or not, but you can only make the most of it if you say goodbye to the old one.
- While an old condition has decayed, you are refusing to see the boat that will carry you to a fresh and inviting new shore. But you haven't missed the boat. It's still waiting for you to step into it.
- Don't get stuck in mourning. Feel your feelings, but look around and see the beautiful opportunities that are here too.
- Be honest about what has rotted and decayed in your life so that you can use it as fertilizer for your fields and fuel for the fire of positive change.
- You are finally ready to emerge from mourning, and to move on.
- Stop hoarding conditions, relationships, or objects. Acknowledge what is past its expiration date, and let it go.
- Breathe into fear and transform it into exhilaration and excitement. Dance with death and find the adventure in change.

14. TEMPERANCE

DIVINE CALIBRATION

GUIDANCE

Call in divine energy to establish balance and harmony within and without. Fine-tune your health, habits, relationships, and environment. Be moderate, temperate, and wise.

In this dynamic, ever-changing current of life, you are constantly learning, growing, and evolving. New information is always flowing in, asking you to let go of old beliefs and upgrade your way of seeing, thinking, behaving, and interacting with the world.

Relax and look within, and you will know what needs to be gently recalibrated. Invoke divine support; imagine the sun and moon shining their balancing light into your energy field and entire life experience. Breathe deeply and allow yourself to see how you can further establish just the right mix of polarities, such as work and play, socialization and solitude, action and rest.

DYNAMICS

The alchemist is concerned with divine harmony. By working with the alchemical elements, the elements of nature, the sun, the moon, thoughts, emotions, habits, and expectations, the alchemist seeks to find the perfect blend. The alchemist further knows that this formula is not static, but active and dynamic — much like the tides and weather patterns that are constantly dancing across the surface of the earth, manipulating and redistributing temperatures, water levels, and resources.

By calling on divine support and allowing sacred wisdom to flow in, you will know what needs to be adjusted, and you will see—in your mind's eye or with your heart—how you can establish the balance that will support your freedom and nourish your soul.

You might not see the whole journey, but you will certainly see your very next step.

SECRETS

Twin priestesses are pouring wine into the sacred lake at sunrise, so it can return to its origin as pure water: the water of life. There is nothing wrong with wine in and of itself, but there was too much of it, so they are performing a loving ritual of healing, offering up what is not needed to the healing and life-giving waters of the earth. This is not wasteful, for they are not throwing the wine away, but giving it to Spirit and allowing it to be transformed, knowing that the living wisdom of the lake will rearrange its molecular structure for the highest and truest good of all.

On the left, we see symbols for the alchemical elements of sulfur, salt, and mercury. On the right, there is the symbol for distillation: the evaporation that creates perfect purity while distributing water around the planet as condensation, clouds, and precipitation. When the light shines through the mist of distillation, it reveals a rainbow, an affirmation of the harmony that comprises the manifest world. The alchemists saw each color of the visible spectrum as being associated with a particular musical note, which formed creation with the essential emanations of sound, tone, and vibration.

The waning moon is reminding you to let go, and its shadow reminds you to be honest about your hidden intentions and what is no longer working for you, as well as what will benefit from gentle and loving correction now.

The single, thornless red rose is a reminder of what we can achieve through intentional cultivation and the highest vibration of all, which is love.

MEANINGS AND MESSAGES OF TEMPERANCE:

- Come into greater balance.
- Ask for and follow divine guidance about how to establish harmony within and without.
- Universal energies support you in letting go of a habit that no longer serves you.
- Proactively fine-tune your world through cleaning, clutter clearing, or enforcing positive health habits.

- Drink plenty of water, eat fruits and vegetables, and be mindfully attentive to what your body needs.
- Meditate and pray every day.
- Masterfully establish beauty in your inner and outer worlds.
- Take care of your personal energy with self-care activities like exercising, spending time in nature, receiving a massage or energy healing, or taking a bath.

MEANINGS AND MESSAGES OF TEMPERANCE — REVERSED:

- Stop ignoring your inner nudge to establish greater balance.
- You're out of balance, but you don't have to fix this alone: ask for help and allow yourself to receive it.
- It may seem impossible to break a habit that no longer serves you, but it isn't. Seek out the help you need in both visible and invisible realms, and you will find it.
- Your environment or habits need some work, and you know it. Stop procrastinating, and take care of yourself now.
- Lovingly acknowledge the habits making it difficult for you to feel good and hear your inner guidance. Then, invoke divine help and take steps to change them right away.
- Prioritize and enforce a daily spiritual practice so you can attune and recalibrate to Spirit regularly.
- Establish beauty and order in your inner monologue and outer world.
- Stop neglecting self-care.

15. THE DEVIL

CALL TO LIBERATE

GUIDANCE

Free yourself from unhealthy dependence on a person, situation, behavior, or substance. Doing so may seem impossible, but it is in fact within your power. When you liberate yourself from this habit or addiction, you will find freedom.

While it's natural and even necessary to rely on external resources and relationships, there are times in every life when we abuse them, use them to numb out, or employ them as a crutch. We overindulge, give away our authority, or believe that we cannot function without something that may have started out innocuously but has unwittingly become a vice.

Be honest about what you need to disengage from or cut back on. Request divine support and humbly enlist the human help and guidance that will serve you best. Once you do this, your way forward will be clear. You won't see the whole path, but you will certainly see how to proceed in this moment and every moment to come, one step and one day at a time.

D Y N A M I C S

Some addictions are obvious and expected — like gambling, alcohol, or drugs. But you can rely on anything to an unhealthy degree. For example, you can get overly caught up in religion, friendship, or work. You can even get so fixated on a hobby that you neglect your relationships and fail to take care of yourself attentively. While you need food, you might get obsessed with eating too much or too little, or you might take nutritional rules too far, counting every calorie and nutrient until you have become painfully untethered from all that makes life wonderful.

In some cases, you must sever ties to a habit or substance utterly, but in other cases, total abstinence is not an option, or is not the best option. For example, no matter how fraught your relationship with food may be, you need food to live. Similarly, you cannot forsake all human contact, and while some relationships may indeed need to be terminated, others will need to be adjusted, calibrated, and healed.

This is your opportunity to break free. Intense power is bound up in whatever you are relying on and whatever you are running from. Cut the cords, face your fear, and reclaim your divine right to thrive.

S E C R E T S

The nonbinary deity Hermaphroditus is represented with both sun and moon faces, the polarities of masculine and feminine present in perfect balance within. The *Ohm* or omega symbol represents the endless and naturally regenerating energy created from the tension of these polarities. Hermaphroditus' internally revitalizing power is yours, but it is temporarily bound by these red cords and the illusion of the devil figure that towers above.

But look closely and see that the cords are simply string and are, in fact, easily breakable. What's more, the Devil is an illusion built on fear. He has no real essence. When you break the cords by overcoming your fear, the Devil's gown will fall, and he will dissolve utterly, returning to his native state of nonbeing.

The winged eye is your angelic nature and your ability to truly see. Look, now, through this eye. See what is real and helpful and what is false and unhelpful. Know what you need to know, step out of your bondage, and be who you have been all along: a divine being, infinitely worthy and burning with dynamic and self-sustaining fire.

MEANINGS AND MESSAGES OF THE DEVIL:

- Release and heal from an addiction or addictive behavior.
- Allow yourself to see what you are using to numb out, then ask for divine and human help with cutting back and getting back on track.
- Be honest about what you have been running from or refusing to admit. Then, be brave. Invoke divine support and face your fear head-on.

- A positive transformation will occur when you heal an addiction, obsession, or emotional imbalance.
- Great power is here for you, but first, you must free yourself from whatever falsely appears to have you in its thrall.
- A relationship with a person, situation, or substance is dysfunctional or codependent. Take steps to fix this.
- You have been handing your power over to something or someone. This is a nudge and an opportunity to reclaim it.

MEANINGS AND MESSAGES OF THE DEVIL — REVERSED:

- You have successfully released an addiction or healed an addictive behavior.
- Spirit has recently intervened in your life to help you reclaim your power over a condition, relationship, or behavior.
- You have bravely admitted your problem or faced your fear, and now you are free.
- A positive transformation has been unlocked through your honesty and courageous action.
- You have successfully reclaimed your power.
- You have recently ended an unhealthy relationship with a person, situation, or substance.
- You have heard and heeded your inner guidance to reclaim your power. Acknowledge and celebrate this accomplishment.

16. THE TOWER
EXTREME DISSOLUTION

GUIDANCE

An unexpected upheaval changes everything. Surrender your ego by letting go of all you can't control and all that is not authentic to you. Destruction makes way for revolution.

Unstable structures must be leveled before you can rebuild. What may have served you in the past becomes unworkable. First, cracks are revealed, and then everything falls apart. In the moment, this can be traumatic, but with time, you will see the necessity of it. When an old building is beyond repair, it must be demolished and removed.

No matter how dramatic this juncture may appear, welcome it, for it is a harbinger of fabulous possibility. Honor your feelings and have compassion for yourself and everyone else as you weather the chaos. But also look forward with joyful expectation to all the beautiful new conditions that are certainly in the works.

D Y N A M I C S

Storms destroy but are necessary for the forest and all its creatures to thrive. Wrecking balls are blunt instruments, but without their use, condemned buildings would proliferate, harboring toxic conditions, posing grave dangers, and preventing the construction of fresh and modern new homes, schools, businesses, and places of healing.

Similarly, life will present you with calamitous and catastrophic problems that are, in fact, perfect opportunities to recognize and demolish old beliefs, concepts, and habits, so you can become free of your ego and egoic illusions and live the life that will satisfy your soul.

Embarrassment can force you to release conceit. Fear can show you how to embrace courage. Loss can open your heart to all the beauty you've experienced and all that you still possess.

When the tower falls, you get to ask, "What will I rebuild in its place?"

S E C R E T S

On the left, the astrological symbol for Aquarius, which is the alchemical symbol for multiplication, moves down into the astrological symbol for Cancer, which is the alchemical symbol for dissolution. What has multiplied beyond what was healthy now dissolves. The ego, or the illusion built from all that is not authentic to your true self, gives way to its native nothingness, making way for who you really are — divine consciousness in temporary human form.

This ego dissolution is also portrayed in the top of the tower breaking away. The false roles and concepts you have bought into about your own personality are no longer tenable, and they are crumbling away forever. While the ego experiences this as a loss, the true self knows that it is a gain. For it is only in losing your false self that you can realize your true identity as infinite consciousness in temporary human form.

As a firestorm of meteoric rain falls from the sky, the tower yields nourishment in perfect balance for the hungriest citizens — aspects of your very self that have previously been marginalized and neglected. The cool, white milk of the mercurial moon and the hot, red blood of the sulfury sun flow from the broken tower, providing what is needed for your evolution and your spiritual path.

Out of great disharmony, great harmony is born.

MEANINGS AND MESSAGES OF THE TOWER:

- Chaotic destruction has appeared in response to the need for comprehensive change.
- Be compassionate with yourself as you move through this crisis, and be assured that beautiful new conditions will follow in its wake.
- Willingly release attachment to your ideas of who you are and who you should be.
- Allow conceit and entitlement to dissolve so you can flow with the changes gracefully and discover the great blessings that will be born in their wake.

- Proactively destroy an old condition to make room for a new one.
- You must endure temporary pain for long-term gain.
- Upheaval is unavoidable. So, see the big picture and welcome the opportunities that will surely come along with this sweeping change.

MEANINGS AND MESSAGES OF THE TOWER — REVERSED:

- Resisting change will only serve to keep you stuck.
- You are in denial about what is in flux. Let yourself see what can never be the same as it once was, and let it dissolve away.
- Stop holding on to your ego out of fear. You will feel free when you finally let your false ideas about yourself go.
- Into every life, a little meteoric fire rain must fall. No matter how hard you try, you can't prevent chaos, shock, or revolutionary change. So, stop screaming at the sky and surrender to the storm.
- You are trying to reinforce what must, in fact, be demolished.
- Seeking to avoid temporary discomfort or pain will prevent you from healing or evolving in the most ideal ways.
- You are stuck in the mourning stage, and this is preventing you from seeing all the new opportunities and blessings that surround you. Honor your feelings, but don't stay mired in negativity forever.

17. THE STAR

THE UNIVERSAL ELIXIR

G U I D A N C E

Spiritual renewal is washing over you. Healing is in effect. Hope is here.

Can you feel it? Your soul is receiving a magical transfusion from the earth, the moon, dreams, beauty, and the pristine waters of the world. Your heart is immersed in the endless wellspring of divine love. You are being reborn, refreshed, reawakened, and buoyed along by the dynamic alchemy of elements in balance: the cool, nourishing, liquid light of the Star.

When the Star shines its replenishing light into your reading, make a wish. Or recognize the wish that is about to be fulfilled — that is even now manifesting into form.

D Y N A M I C S

While this is a card of granted wishes, it is not about final outcomes and happy-ever-afters, but of the endless flow of harmony you can tap into on every point on the wheel of time.

The Star will not show you every step or reveal every secret. But, if you allow it, it will show you just what you need to know, just when you need to know it. It's a living current of energy that will spiral and swirl into your life experience in an endless flow. It is the universal elixir that will allow you to renew yourself utterly: to heal, balance, harmonize, bless your life and life conditions, and flow toward your most ideal success.

The light of the Star is one single, collective ray, but it shines and makes itself available through many channels. Just as the woman in this image reaches for the star that is most accessible to her, look to the wisdom that is already there for you. Seize the opportunity that is right in front of your eyes.

The Star reminds you that you are precious, magical, and divine, just as you are today. Instead of chasing a sense of superiority or attempting to elevate yourself above the fray, find common ground and recognize your similarities with others while simultaneously celebrating the things that make you unique. Find the ordinary within the extraordinary and the miraculous within the everyday.

S E C R E T S

Notice that one foot is on the earth and the other is in the pond. Staying in the realm of the earthy and practical, concurrently stand in the fluid realm of memories, intuitions, and dreams. This borderland is where healing and magic live.

Similarly, healing requires us to tend to our mind, body, and spirit — separately but also as one. In alchemy, this is symbolized by the balance of alchemical elements: mercury, sulfur, and salt.

One of her pitchers, the woman has already emptied. The other, she is emptying now. In this same vein, acknowledge and honor your feelings. Let them flow and let them go.

Also, recognize and then release all that you cannot change. Like pouring out your cares and worries into a sacred spring of liquid light, release the futile desire to control the things you can't control. This is how you will access the transcendent, resplendent, transformative power of the Star.

MEANINGS AND MESSAGES OF THE STAR:

- Profound healing is taking place for you.
- A wish is being fulfilled or is about to be fulfilled.
- Listen to the wisdom that is already present within you.
- Positive transformation is underway.
- Enjoy the journey.
- Open to new possibilities. Dare to claim what you truly want.
- Flow with time as one big, endless spiral of light.
- Continue tending to your wellness: mind, body, and spirit.
- After a period of convalescence, mourning, or retreat, you are ready to return to daily activities, community, and the outside world.

MEANINGS AND MESSAGES OF THE STAR — REVERSED:

- Healing is here for you, but you must be willing to allow it. Follow your intuition about how to release blocks.
- Don't set your sights on the perpetually inaccessible. Look for opportunities that are closer and more available. You can always expand into even more blessings later.
- External messages conflict. Relax, breathe, and listen to the still, small voice within.
- Don't try to do everything at once. Slow down and find joy in every step.
- Don't limit yourself by pessimism or expectations of lack.
- Ask yourself: *WHAT IF?* ... *What if* the universe is on my side? *What if* I'm not finite, but eternal? *What if* I already know exactly what I need to know? *What if* I already have everything I need? What does it look like? How does it feel?
- Tune in to the self-care you need. Let go of habits that harm you, diminish you, or drain away your power.
- You can't hide away forever. Retreat has its place, but now you must make the effort to return.

18. THE MOON

DARKNESS OF THE WOMB

GUIDANCE

The big picture is hidden, or the truth is obscured. Someone's hiding something, or a mystery remains unsolved. Beware of dishonesty, illusion, or subterfuge, or simply allow time, patience, and your intuitive gifts to reveal what you need to know.

In this earthly existence, we cannot and should not know everything at once. Like a novel or a dramatic film, there are points in the narrative when we must wonder and wait. This is one of those points. You may think you have all the information you need, but you don't. So be sure to take a moment to pause, observe, and investigate more fully before you blindly jump in.

Even if someone is not deliberately deceiving you, everything is not as it appears. Take this in stride. Listen to your intuition and surrender the need for obvious or immediate answers.

DYNAMICS

The Moon is Diana, and her realm is a shadowy and moonlit sanctuary for wolves, witches, outlaws, fortune tellers, and thieves: those who deal in secrets and operate under the cover of night.

While we must construct stories to make sense of our world, none of these stories are ever precisely accurate or true. The best we can hope is that they approximate the truth in such a way as to be useful. But we must recognize when our stories need to be reworked. It's possible that you've been operating under a story that is not accurate enough to be of practical assistance. Examine your assumptions and acknowledge the working models that could be leading you in circles or carrying you so far into the darkness that you lose sight of the light.

SECRETS

Diana is the goddess of the moon, and her realm is the earth and the physical world. In alchemy, she is silver, which the alchemists combined with mercury and gold in such a way to form a tiny dendritic tree, called Diana's Tree. This appeared with branches like fruiting grain, and was believed to be a forerunner of the philosopher's stone.

In a lesser-known version of the Eleusinian myth, Diana appeared to the goddess Persephone (along with Venus and Athena), to escort her directly to Pluto, where she could fulfill her role as the queen of death and the underworld, and in turn facilitate eternal life and the perennial rebirth of spring.

Diana's contribution was the knowledge that, at times, secrets and mysteries are required. We must make friends with the shadowy netherworld and abide there for a time, if we are to effectively herald the return of the light.

A symbol of the womb is at her belly — a reminder that gestation occurs in the dark. In entering Diana's womblike realm, you will evolve in the darkness until your understanding is fully formed and you are ready to be reborn into the light.

MEANINGS AND MESSAGES OF THE MOON:

- There is something that is not yet entirely clear to you. Wait and observe until more comes into view.
- Someone is deceiving you, or you don't yet have all the information you need.
- Take time to rest and reflect before moving forward, and more will be revealed.
- Examine your assumptions and paradigms. Root out what may not be in alignment with what is real, useful, or true.
- Even though you may prefer to take swift and decisive action, you will be wise to wait until you know more.
- Get comfortable with the mystery and find refuge in the shadows. Our psychic and intuitive gifts often speak to us in riddles and symbols, refusing to be obvious or concrete.
- Engage in shadow work: get honest about the aspects of your psyche you aren't proud of or wish you could escape.
- Consult your intuition and trust your inner knowing, even if it doesn't reveal everything at once.

MEANINGS AND MESSAGES OF THE MOON — REVERSED:

- A period of confusion has ended. You are finally able to see the way out of the dark.
- A deception has been uncovered or a mystery has been solved.
- Don't get stuck in reflection or rumination. You've done your due diligence — now act.
- You have successfully shifted an unhelpful paradigm, and you are now poised to move forward into greater success.
- The wait is over. You have the information you need.
- Listen to your intuition. It is there for you, but you must trust it. Relax, get still, invoke divine support, and you will discover you indeed know what to do.
- Don't ignore your shadow. Ask, "What aspects of this challenge are familiar, and how might I take some responsibility for what I am experiencing?"
- While it's true that you can't predict what the whole journey will look like, your intuition is showing you your very next step.

19. THE SUN

THE PHILOSOPHER'S STONE

GUIDANCE

The sun is shining on you. All that you need, the universe is offering to you. Your way forward is gloriously illuminated, and your abundant good fortune is here.

The luckiest of lucky cards, the Sun affirms that you are on the right path and that all the power of heaven is here to support you. Everything is clicking. You are in the flow. You are a magnet to blessings. Lavish wealth is coming to you. All that you seek is seeking you.

Smile and relax, knowing your prosperity is part of the divine plan. This is a time when your guidance is clear and easy to hear, so you need only follow it. Effortless, shining momentum is on the horizon for you. You have much to enjoy and much to happily anticipate.

If you're wondering if a project, avenue, or opportunity will reap rewards, take this as a yes.

If you have been going through a challenge, celebrate, for your struggle is finally ending. The clouds of discord are parting. The golden sun of luck is reasserting itself and gloriously illuminating your sky.

Rich and beautiful blessings are here for you now, and even more are on the way.

DYNAMICS

Luck is what happens when inner work, outer work, divine resonance, and worldly opportunity combine. You meditate, learn, pray, work, build, believe in yourself, and watch for possibilities, and then the heavens open and the light of good fortune shines. This is the philosopher's stone: the golden favor of the cosmos that comes to the alchemist who does the great work.

For those who are diligent and show up for this work again and again throughout their lifetime, such portals of good fortune appear not just once, but repeatedly, at intervals, in an upward spiral of light. For the committed alchemist, this is a lifelong process of leveling up.

SECRETS

This prince appears here as two princes, but he is, in truth, one. We are glimpsing his higher self lovingly and decisively leading his earthly or visible self forward toward victory. By doing the spiritual work that has brought his conscious mind into harmony with his divine mind, these aspects are cooperating perfectly, and this fortuitous partnership is opening the way for and lending momentum to the prince's success. He has earned his crown, which hovers above him, blessed by and imbued with the infinite light of the sun.

The circle is the prince's conscious mind, the sun is his divine mind, and the sign for amalgamation indicates the work that he has done to unify the two. What's more, the moon appears on the horizon to show that he has successfully integrated his receptive, lunar self with his active, solar self. In fact, he has combined his inner forces so masterfully that he has won the alchemist's grandest prize. In transforming the base metals of consciousness into spiritual gold, he has obtained the glorious crown that is the philosopher's stone. This brings inner and outer wealth.

MEANINGS AND MESSAGES OF THE SUN:

- Success is here.
- You are in luck.
- The object of your inquiry is destined to succeed.
- A portal of golden opportunity is open.
- Your struggle is over. Peace, joy, and good fortune are here.
- Divinity is orchestrating your success.
- You have done the work, and now you may reap the rewards.
- Money and resources are coming to you in abundance.
- Your generosity has unlocked the riches of heaven.
- The sun is shining on you in response to your inner and outer work. Bask in the glory and celebrate all that you've achieved.

MEANINGS AND MESSAGES OF THE SUN — REVERSED:

- Success is here, but you must allow yourself to see it.
- A lucky opportunity is waiting for you — notice and seize it.
- You can experience the success you desire (and soon), but you must believe in yourself.
- Don't just walk through this portal of opportunity nonchalantly — also celebrate your good fortune, acknowledge your hard work, and give thanks to the Divine.
- Release fear and allow yourself to trust that the hard parts of your journey are behind you.
- Divine orchestration is here, but it's slightly blocked. To unblock it, all you need to do is relax and allow your good fortune to flow with ease.
- You have achieved something spectacular, but haven't taken the time to enjoy it yet.
- Cultivate a sense of ease around wealth. Relax and receive it. Be assured that you deserve it, and prosperity is your birthright.
- As you receive the blessings that are coming to you, notice and release any guilt that may arise. There's plenty for everyone. Remember that when you have more, it doesn't diminish the success or abundance of others.
- Acknowledging your good fortune is a secret key to leveling up. Don't overlook it.

20. JUDGMENT
THE GODS INTERVENE

GUIDANCE

You are a key player in a grand mythic cycle. Be transformed in the underworld of your past challenges and rise anew. Embrace and fulfill your destiny, for unstoppable karmic forces are at work.

This is an epic calling and a hero's journey. Expect a startling realization, a demanding rite of passage, or a radical transformation that is beyond your ability to mitigate or control.

The seeds of this challenge or situation were planted long ago, and their roots go deep. It's possible that you are dealing with something that started with your ancestors or in a past life. It's also likely that, in this present life, you can perceive a past action or choice that set these present events in motion. Or perhaps you've repeatedly faced a similar challenge in a different form.

Whatever the origin, you have been granted an opportunity to face this old pattern courageously, rise out of the underworld of struggle and paralysis, and be reborn.

DYNAMICS

Even though you appear to be a small and temporary being, aimlessly wandering the surface of the earth, you are in fact eternal, and your consciousness is one with the Divine. Sometimes, this larger consciousness appears to intervene, vigorously rearranging your circumstances and propelling your life forward as part of a grander pattern and path. Some call it a "bolt from the blue." In myths and narratives, it is a *Deus ex Machina*, a "machine of the gods": an occurrence that brings swift respite or all-encompassing change, and that can only be attributed to the mysterious workings of fate, heaven, and the vast unknown.

The goddess Persephone was abducted by Hades, the god of the underworld. On the surface, the myth appears to describe a random act of violence. Indeed, Persephone's mother, Demeter, protests and laments what Hades has done. But the deeper and more authentic telling of the myth reveals that Persephone knew her destiny and embraced it. Without her descent into the underworld, there could be no autumn or winter, and as the goddess of spring, she well knew that all seasons are needed for the daffodils (and all the other plants) to grow.

SECRETS

The golden wheat is rising from Persephone's body, clearly showing her mythic cycle to be essential, bringing life and sustenance to the world. She has surrendered completely, knowing that without this period of underworld immersion, she can't fulfill her role as the goddess of rebirth and verdant spring.

At the bottom of the triangle is the sign for salt: the alchemist's symbol for the human body and tangible world. Above the earth, the glyphs for mercury and sulfur hover, showing the dynamic transformation from matter to spirit, and the combination of the three to form all that we experience and see.

Above the wheat, we see the symbol for stone. Above that, there is the symbol for life. From the seemingly inert, new life is born.

Above, we see an angelic orb, where every feather is an eye. This is the divine consciousness that oversees all that was, is, and will be.

Heavenly hands reach down from above. They are the *Deus ex Machina*: the grand and startling plot twist decreed by karmic forces and the gods.

MEANINGS AND MESSAGES OF JUDGMENT:

- Destiny is calling to you: heed it.
- Present events were set in motion long ago.
- Heal an ancestral pattern or fulfill a past life contract so you can graduate from this challenge for good.
- This is an opportunity to reinvent yourself or be reborn.
- You may have a powerful desire to change the course of your life in a dramatic or unexpected way. Honor it.
- Present-moment chaos, challenges, and sweeping change are necessary aspects of your life's narrative and trajectory.

- Surrender to your destiny. Face your challenges courageously and you will succeed.

MEANINGS AND MESSAGES OF JUDGMENT — REVERSED:

- Stop ignoring your destiny. Listen to your intuition and let it guide you.
- Don't get so caught up in the moment that you can't see the big picture and find the blessing and lesson in what you are facing.
- Don't keep doing the same thing and expecting a different outcome.
- Stop clinging to the past.
- You are logically overriding and trying to talk yourself out of where your destiny is leading you. Act on your intuition and follow what feels right, even if you don't understand exactly why.
- You are getting too caught up in the drama to see that these challenges are temporary, and they are necessary to your life's most ideal unfolding. Take a step back, see the big picture, and be grateful for the opportunities that present themselves.
- Don't try to change what you can't change. Instead, take a positive perspective and look for opportunities to heal, evolve, and be reborn.

21. THE WORLD

THE END IS THE BEGINNING

GUIDANCE

At the end of a journey, a circle is complete. Everything is different, yet there is also a sense of sameness, even as a new era commences. After going out into the world in search of your fortune, you discovered it buried in the very soil where you began.

You have achieved a significant victory, and you now graduate to a new level of mastery. You started out as the Fool, with no set plan, few belongings, no accolades, and every possible avenue in the ether around you.

Now, your expedition has taken form. Working with the primordial elements, you have built something tangible and painstakingly forged a unique path. Along the way, you have gathered wisdom and experience, and you now contain the whole world within your very self.

As you embark upon or celebrate this final shining moment of your odyssey of self-discovery, you must continue to be brave. Finish victoriously. Don't hesitate to follow the clear nudges and messages you are receiving from the Infinite Consciousness, which are being communicated directly to your mind, body, heart, and soul.

This card may indicate an obvious achievement like buying your first house or sending a child off to college. Or it could be pointing to something more internal, like finally learning to love yourself, healing from an addiction, or achieving a new level of mastery in your interpersonal relationships.

DYNAMICS

The 22 cards of the Major Arcana begin with the Fool and conclude with the World. The Fool has been through a lot. During their travels, they have become a master. They are now the World — the mother of everything. The mother need not continue to wander aimlessly or scurry from place to place. She is grounded, rooted, and at peace, for she knows that wherever she is, she has access to the entire world and all it contains.

There is a sense of destiny fulfilled, as if all along, on some hidden level, you knew this was where you would end up. And even if the physical location or role was here for you the whole time, you couldn't have embodied or enjoyed it properly until you went through every twist and turn along your path. At the time, those twists and turns may have seemed random. But now, they seem perfectly orchestrated to bring you to this luminous end.

And, even as this journey concludes, another has already begun. It's an endlessly regenerating cycle. The World gives birth to the Fool.

SECRETS

The *Animus Mundi* is the soul, or conscious aliveness, of the earth, and all it cradles and contains. You are a part of this soul, and you also contain it within your every cell. The *Animus Mundi* is the eye on the diamond, which the Divine Mother possesses easily, without grasping or needing to hold on.

As the World, your alchemical journey has made you wise. You are purified. You have transformed lead into gold. You have obtained the philosopher's stone.

You have more responsibilities, but they do not weigh you down. They inspire and bless you, and you are perfectly qualified to fulfill them.

Because you have mastered your destiny and your art, the four elements of nature surround you, in perfect harmony. The alchemical elements hover beneath your hand, waiting to be shaped into anything you choose.

MEANINGS AND MESSAGES OF THE WORLD:

- Embrace your destiny and celebrate all that you've achieved.
- Take joy in being the master you have become.
- A cycle has been completed, even as a new one now begins.
- Be brave and trust your inner knowing that all is unfolding as it should.
- There may be just a few more steps, but the end is in sight, so don't stop now.
- You are in a good spot. The World is at your fingertips. You hold the World in your hand.

- You have worked hard and been through a lot to achieve this success. Acknowledge and believe that you deserve it.

MEANINGS AND MESSAGES OF THE WORLD — REVERSED:

- Stop fighting destiny. Admit what you truly desire and be proud of who you are.
- Don't let a setback discourage you. Accept it, learn from it, and move on.
- You may feel like you've backtracked, but now you can learn something even more deeply, which will bring great benefits.
- It feels like things aren't going the way they are supposed to, but there is profound potential for growth in this challenge.
- In time, you will see the divine order in what you are experiencing, even if it presently feels random or chaotic.
- Choose to see the good in this situation, or just to believe it is there. This will transform a fate into a destiny.
- Instead of looking for what's wrong with this moment, look for the opportunities, and trust that things are unfolding as they should.

ACE OF VASES

PURE FLOW

GUIDANCE

This watery ace heralds abundant flow, which may come to you in the form of love, motivation, spirituality, healing, or wealth. This is an omen of luck and a harbinger of something beautiful and new. Expect a deluge of heartfelt blessings — acknowledge them and welcome them in.

A new relationship may be sailing into your life. Or perhaps an existing relationship is evolving in a wonderful way, for example through engagement or another form of enhanced commitment.

You may be presented with a new creative or work project that satisfies your thirst for inspiration and floods your soul with joy.

Perhaps, through meditation, ritual, or study, your spiritual path feels freshly invigorated and renewed.

This card may also indicate successful healing, particularly when you have recently discovered or implemented a new treatment or care strategy.

Or, you may have tapped into a geyser of affluent prosperity.

D Y N A M I C S

Ace of Vases is the water element in its purest and most primordial form. As the first card of the suit, it signifies something pure and fresh, such as an unexpected blessing or a brand-new chapter.

The water element is aligned with the emotions, as well as abundant flow in all its many forms. Water is healing, renewing, and nourishing. It is associated with dreams, creativity, peace, love, cleansing, and wealth.

S E C R E T S

The symbol for the water element is in the upper right corner.

On the left side of the card, we see the symbol for femininity and the planet Venus, for water is the element of the womb and the endless wellspring of love within.

From the heart, sweet grapes grow — they are the essence of love, which quenches our thirst while bringing sustenance and delight to body, mind, and soul.

The flying fish symbolizes a leap of faith: jumping eagerly from the known to the unknown to expand his sense of what is possible before plunging once again into the glittering sea.

Like the fish, the cloud is an entity of water that is also at home in the air. The slower and more downward flow of water is tempered by the buoyancy of air — the element of lightness, inventiveness, and swift movement.

MEANINGS AND MESSAGES OF ACE OF VASES:

- Expect a new and beautiful relationship or expect an existing relationship to evolve in a positive way.
- A new opportunity is flowing in, bringing inspiration, prosperity, and joy.
- Money is coming to you. Your cash flow is opening up.
- A leap of faith will be rewarded.
- A lucky break is on its way.
- Creative or spiritual inspiration is flowing in copiously or is being generously renewed.
- A healing miracle is coming to you.

MEANINGS AND MESSAGES OF ACE OF VASES – REVERSED:

- Don't fear this new relationship. Or stop pushing a loved one away.
- Don't dismiss this opportunity. Give it a chance.
- Heal your relationship with money so you can allow it to flow to you.
- Take steps to calm and align your mind, body, and spirit so you can act from love rather than fear, and take a leap of faith.
- A lucky opportunity is coming, but if you don't look for it or expect it, you might miss it.
- Unblock your creative flow by taking positive action toward your visions and dreams.

- Show up and do the work; in time, your natural motivation will return.
- Don't just wait around wishing and hoping. Commit to taking care of yourself, take guided action, and listen to your intuition about new avenues of success and self-care.

TWO OF VASES

LOVE HEALS

GUIDANCE

A divine partnership is here. A romantic relationship, family relationship, friendship, or business partnership brings blessings. A connection between two people ushers in healing or a new era of positivity and success.

As the two-fold expression of the water element, Two of Vases is an archetypal expression of pure love, and the healing that comes from connecting with someone on an emotional and soul level.

If you're asking about a relationship, this card is validation that there is beautiful potential here. If you're not, allow yourself to know the relationship to which this card refers. Know, also, that it will support you, heal you, and bless you.

DYNAMICS

Here, Venus, the planet of love, resides in Cancer, the sign of the emotions. Tenderness, harmony, beauty, and mutual respect prevail. This is a healthy relationship in which each partner honors the other as an equal and is willing to combine forces to create a collaborative dynamic that is even more powerful than the sum of its parts.

This card meets us in the realm of emotions. Don't ignore your intellect or your gut but consult earnestly with the quality of energy at your heart. Be honest about what your heart knows, even if it appears to contradict the surface appearance of things.

Even though we get caught up in the quest for abundance, respect, and worldly success, love and relationships are what bring us true happiness and infuse our lives with meaning. Feel the joy of connection and let it activate a divine and intuitive flow.

S E C R E T S

The top vase drips *rubedo*, the alchemical substance that helps formulate the philosopher's stone and turn metals into gold. Behind this vase is the sun, which reinforces the vital healing energy that is present in a respectful and loving relationship.

The bottom vase holds a red rose, a most potent symbol of beauty, power, passion, and the highest and purest vibration of love. Behind this vase is a waxing moon, illustrating emotion and the fresh and nourishing quality of two people in a positive partnership and harmonious union.

Together, in their own bubble, the two light beings swim together dreamily, immersed in the healing waters of love.

The sign for Venus is in the ether, and in the upper right corner hangs the symbol for water.

MEANINGS AND MESSAGES OF TWO OF VASES:

- The relationship you are asking about is healthy and sound, or has the potential to be.
- You will receive great healing and blessings from a partnership of some kind.
- Open your heart and be brave so you can connect with another being on a deep level.
- Allow yourself to be seen and loved for who you are, and be sure to see and love another in just the same way.
- Together, you and a partner (romantic or otherwise) will go far.
- Pay attention to the primary relationship related to the object of your inquiry. Take care of it, and it will take care of you.

MEANINGS AND MESSAGES OF TWO OF VASES — REVERSED:

- The relationship you are asking about is temporarily blocked in some way but has the potential to heal.
- If you open your heart and allow yourself to be vulnerable, you will soon discover great healing potential within a relationship that currently seems to be discordant.
- Someone is trying to connect with you, but your fear is keeping you from seeing the lovely and magical person they truly are.

- You are trying to connect with someone, but they are afraid. If you can remain steadfast and earn their trust, you will see a positive shift.
- Stop trying to go it alone. Partner with someone else or allow yourself to receive the help that is offered.

THREE OF VASES

FRIENDLY AND FAMILIAL LOVE

GUIDANCE

The love of family and friends is true abundance. Feel gratitude for your beloved community in all its many forms and gravitate towards your social support system. Look for a reason to celebrate with others or gather simply for the joy of it.

Like a harvest celebration, take time to give thanks for all the sweetness in your life — particularly the people you know and love.

Whatever you're asking about or facing, look for ways to incorporate community. Embark on a business venture with friends, say yes to a party invitation, or reach out to family members for help or advice.

DYNAMICS

When you spend time with people who deeply see and understand you, and when you see and understand them in return, you have a sense that together, you can do anything. And, in many ways, you can. A sense of community blesses you with resilience, agency, and courage. The combined wisdom and talents of the group become like a singular super-intelligence that is greater than the sum of its parts.

The power of such an alliance cannot be overstated. It blesses your health, wealth, and happiness in every possible way.

While duos are wonderful, this card refers to being in community not just with one other person, but with two or more.

S E C R E T S

Together, the women walk across the surface of the water. They can do so because they believe and trust that, jointly, they are all-powerful. And so they are.

Their heads are vases, filled to the brim not with disembodied thought, but with the poignant, lucky, and vital waters of life. Together, their energies flow, combining their essences to make the magic that fills our lives with meaning: laughter, comfort, and the freedom of knowing that no matter where you go in life, your loved ones are on your side. They wish you well and will do everything they can to help you thrive, just as you feel the same way about them.

In the upper right corner, we see the symbol for water. Below the women and to the left, we see the symbol for femininity and the planet Venus.

MEANINGS AND MESSAGES OF THREE OF VASES:

- Make time for friends and/or family. Schedule an outing, organize a dinner party, or attend a gathering.
- The answer to your question lies in community: enlist the help of family or friends or look for ways to contribute to an organization or group.
- Celebrate and give thanks for all the love in your life, and all the friends and family that give you the invaluable feeling of loving and being loved.
- Ask for help with whatever you're doing.
- Make a project into a community effort and a celebration.

MEANINGS AND MESSAGES OF THREE OF VASES – REVERSED:

- Mourn as needed after heartbreak or discord within a family or friend group. When you're ready, open your heart and bravely build a new community or establish a new and healthier dynamic.
- There are others who would love to help you, so stop trying to go it alone. Ask for help from loved ones or take steps to build a community around your goal.
- You may feel heartbroken or empty because of loneliness or past challenges in your relationships with family or friends. Honor those feelings, but then look for the love you already have in your life and give thanks for it. Then, proactively find and cultivate a loving group of like-minded folks.

- Don't let a sense of vulnerability deter you from asking for help. Override reluctance, and you will be rewarded with generous support. Remember that people love to help.
- You are being too solitary and serious about your goal — try making it a group effort or a party instead.

FOUR OF VASES
BOUT OF BOREDOM

G U I D A N C E

Reconnect with your gratitude and your joy. Move your body, open your heart, and unblock the flow of your passion. Beautiful opportunities are being offered to you, but they still await your recognition.

It's natural to encounter brief periods of boredom. At times, we all feel closed off, grouchy, or spaced out. While we would of course prefer a constant state of flow, our hearts sometimes seem to turn off the lights and lock the door. We begin to believe that life is far less fabulous and wonderful than it is.

This is a nudge, however, to get yourself out of this rut. While you dwell in the physical world, you are a spiritual being. You are a creature of the cosmos: infinite, mystical, and brilliant. Stop overidentifying with only that which you can touch, quantify, and see. Let the mysterious and ineffable magic of being flow back into your consciousness, get you back on your feet, and propel you upward into joy.

DYNAMICS

You may have become so contented with the status quo that you have forgotten to try new things or brave the world outside your comfort zone. Openheartedness may have begun to feel vulnerable for you. Having been hurt in the past, it's possible you inadvertently shut the doors of your heart to avoid feeling such pain ever again. While this may succeed in preventing conscious and acute emotional discomfort, it will also numb you out and separate you from your joy.

Try something new. Challenge yourself. Perform a ritual and invoke the Divine. Move, dance, and take walks outside. Breathe consciously and set the intention to re-sensitize yourself to magic. Invoke, look for, and be receptive to all the love in the world.

SECRETS

The water of abundant joy is falling from the heavens, but the figure in the image is upside down. His head is a rock, balanced on three other rocks. These rocks are stable, but their inert nature means they possess no mysterious possibilities.

While balance is generally a good thing, too much of it can become stagnant, keeping us in a dreary thrall.

Still, while his head is temporarily frozen in its solidness, his body remembers that he is a creature of the stars. His body holds the secret to reanimating his mind and reconnecting his thoughts with his feelings and his heart.

MEANINGS AND MESSAGES OF FOUR OF VASES:

- Open your heart by challenging yourself, moving your body, and engaging in activities that inspire you.
- Just because you like where you are, it doesn't mean you can't explore new possibilities and do things in new ways.
- Your boredom is feeding on itself, causing you to see things as less wonderful than they are. Breathe into your heart, inhabit your body, and look at a relationship or an opportunity through fresh eyes.
- It's time for a shakeup. Be willing to be unsettled or out of balance for a while for the sake of inspiration, adventure, and present-moment joy.
- Even a little change can spark positive results: switch up your hairstyle, listen to new music, wear a color you don't normally wear, or take a different route to work.

MEANINGS AND MESSAGES OF FOUR OF VASES — REVERSED:

- You have emotionally and spiritually shut down in response to a sense of overwhelm. Stop overscheduling yourself, take some time off, and reduce stress by lightening your outlook and your load.
- Stop trying to do everything by yourself. Allow help from the Divine and other people.

- Build moments of contemplation, relaxation, and play into your schedule so you can open your heart and recalibrate your joy.
- You are overbooked and overburdened. If everything comes crashing down, let it be an opportunity to rebuild your outlook and schedule in a more sustainable way.
- Don't let your life get so predictable that you never dare to venture out into the unexpected and the wild unknown.

FIVE OF VASES

FROM PAIN TO HEALING

G U I D A N C E

This is a message of comfort and healing after profound heartbreak and loss. Breathe deeply into your pain even as you know that it will, in time, surely fade. Not only will your heart mend, but you will also become stronger, wiser, and more receptive to joy.

To heal pain, you must first feel it. You must be brave and let it take as long as it takes.

But remember — even when it seems as if your suffering will go on forever, that is never the case. While you may always harbor a certain wistful and nostalgic ache, when it comes to acute emotional agony, this, too, shall pass.

Take care of yourself as best you can. Treat yourself to warm baths, walks outside, healthy food, and comforting music. Seek out support as you are guided from friends, family, counselors, healers, and mental health professionals.

As you repair your heart and emotions and treat yourself like the precious creature you are, you will increase your capacity for compassion, wonder, understanding, and depth.

While no one wants to suffer, at the same time, healers, artists, and alchemists all know there is value in disappointment, grief, and emotional wounding.

DYNAMICS

Every life contains heartache. Every deep relationship requires presence and, at times, demands that we experience pain.

The alchemist doesn't shrink from her grief but uses it. Through meticulous attention and care, she channels it into freedom and invites it into the great work of transforming the base metals of everyday challenges into shining spiritual gold.

The wisest people are those who have known grief. The most joyful people are those who have known sorrow.

SECRETS

These vases are filled with tears, heavy with heartache. As they fall and are released, a yellow parakeet climbs up and out. This is emotional freedom, breaking free, and preparing to soar upward, toward the eternal center of her sparkling, sunlit joy.

Along with the vases, we see the symbol for copper and the planet Venus: emotional pain comes with profound beauty. As we release the pain, the beauty does not dissolve or disappear, for it is eternal.

In the upper right corner, we see the symbol for water.

Beneath the portal to the cosmos, we see tears: drops of a saltwater potion that cleanses the heart and soul.

MEANINGS AND MESSAGES OF FIVE OF VASES:

- Your pain won't last forever. Feel it so you can heal it and let it go.
- Be proactive in your healing. Be kind to yourself and lovingly tend to your needs.
- Enlist the help of friends, family, healers, and counselors as you feel guided. Allow them to support you, and to simply be present to offer their love.
- Remember that everyone experiences emotional suffering in this lifetime. We are creatures who love deeply; deep love comes with profound suffering.
- You are not alone. Let an awareness of the universality of suffering offer you some degree of comfort.
- Look back, and you will see how your suffering taught you important lessons and expanded your capacity for joy.

MEANINGS AND MESSAGES OF FIVE OF VASES — REVERSED:

- You are already healing. Patiently honor your experience as you breathe deeply and continue to heal.
- Don't neglect your everyday needs. Take loving care of yourself and offer yourself kindness and comfort.
- Don't suffer alone. Ask for help.
- Be careful not to become isolated, or to believe that no one else has felt this way before. Remember that everyone suffers.
- Seek out support and comfort from others.

- Don't fight or deny what happened. Accept it and remember that no matter how heartbreaking a challenge is, it will contain hidden blessings and opportunities to grow.

SIX OF VASES
LOVE IS SIMPLE

GUIDANCE

Abundance, happiness, and healing are here for you if you will but stop and notice. Smell the flowers, soak in the beauty, and inhabit the now. Home is found in everyday moments of interconnection and peace.

Disappointment can give way to happiness when you realize that what you seek isn't outside of what you already have. In searching for, and not quite obtaining, the worldly glamor or success you thought you wanted, you finally learn how blessed and lucky you were from the beginning.

Simplicity is the shining star at the innermost heart of all that is. All the joy one could possibly hope for can be found in acknowledging a true friend, a family member who accepts you no matter what, a shared laugh over a glowing memory, and the beauty of a single flower in your own backyard.

DYNAMICS

We can often make things more complicated than they are. We pick up the idea that we need a certain degree of prosperity or recognition to be satisfied, or that we will only feel right once we've obtained a certain item, reached a certain milestone, or arranged things in our home just so.

While there's nothing wrong with amassing objects, racking up accomplishments, and meticulously decorating our spaces, Six of Vases brings us back to ourselves. We are reminded that such things are only truly enjoyable when they are nourished by a core of knowing that we already have enough and we already are enough, and we are therefore already rich.

At the end of your life, you will look back on the sweetest memories — those born of simple connection and present-moment love. All the rest will pale in comparison to these. So, revel now in the abundance that already surrounds you, fills you, and radiates from the center of your heart.

SECRETS

This young girl is both human and rose: a hybrid of two beings on Earth with the potential to vibrate at the highest frequency of all, which is love. Love heals. Love makes judgment dissolve utterly and fall away. Love keeps our attention on the truest aspect of ourselves and others, which is divine, eternal, blameless, and transcendent.

Simply invoking and recalling the scent and appearance of a rose purifies your mind, body, and spirit, attuning you to the pure love that illuminates the present, blesses the future, and drenches your memories in the brightest light.

When a memory of a time or relationship is purely sweet, it is not less accurate, but more. The illusions of discord have fallen away, leaving only what is, was, and ever shall be real: love.

MEANINGS AND MESSAGES OF SIX OF VASES:

- Attune to the frequency of love.
- Be fully present in the now.
- Gaze at the past and present through eyes of love.
- Approach this situation with the true forgiveness and acceptance born of divine love.
- Preciousness already surrounds you. Place your awareness on it and soak it in.
- Play, open your heart, and expand into childlike innocence.
- Simplify this situation by focusing on love.

MEANINGS AND MESSAGES OF SIX OF VASES – REVERSED:

- You are making things more complicated than they need to be. Focus on love and let everything else fall away.

- Enjoy what's here for you in this moment. You can remember the past and anticipate the future while also fully inhabiting the now.
- Instead of looking for the problems and imperfections, raise your awareness to the transcendent truth of love.
- When you stop judging others and holding grudges, you will find more freedom for yourself and forgive your own mistakes.
- You are already lucky and rich, but you have temporarily forgotten to notice. This is a loving reminder.
- Your inner child has been cooped up for too long. Let her play.

SEVEN OF VASES

WISE CHOICE

GUIDANCE

Assess where you are, where you've been, and where you're going. Gather wisdom, seek clarity, and integrate the choices and experiences that have brought you to this point. Get clear on your values, goals, and intentions so you can make a wise decision about what to do next.

You have been through challenges, and you have enriched your wisdom. Pain has made you stronger and more compassionate. Friends, guides, practices, perspectives, and spiritual resources each swirl their own brand of resilience and insight into the potion of your awareness and being.

But ultimately, you are the alchemist, and you must decide not just what you want to create, but also how you want to create it.

Your destiny awaits. But you must be an active participant in bringing it into form. Without decisive action, it will remain ethereal and unrealized.

Steady your mind. Contemplate. Consider. Consult your intellect while also taking your emotions and passions into account.

Then, act.

DYNAMICS

One can wish and wash without being wishy-washy. The water element, which is the realm of dreams and emotions, can mire you in indecision, but it can also be employed to help you envision what you want, cleanse your life of what you don't want, and thrive.

Seven of Cups is a reminder that without intention and action—without decisively choosing one option or path at the exclusion of all others—passions will remain latent, goals unreached, and dreams unrealized.

There is a time to gather wisdom. There is a time to imagine what is possible. And there is a time, eventually, to act. Now is the time to act.

SECRETS

Seven of Vases is Venus in Scorpio: beauty and love as alchemy. What wisdom and experience can you strategically combine to create a fabulous future? How can you take what you have learned and make it into magic?

The emotional waters of love want to flow. Don't let your fondest dreams stagnate in the dark. Act decisively and let them pour onward like a glorious mountain stream, gleaming and sparkling in the sun.

The large vase at the bottom is you. The five vases above it hold all the many preferences and experiences that have defined you and brought you to this point. As the contents of the vases combine into the potion of your destiny, the eye of providence watches.

There is great significance in your action now — not just for you, but also for the living sea of consciousness that holds all that is, was, and shall be.

MEANINGS AND MESSAGES OF SEVEN OF VASES:

- Feel your feelings, consult your wisdom, assess where you've been, and decide where you want to go. Then, with great determination, act.
- This choice profoundly affects your destiny.
- You have everything you need to make a wise choice.
- Take passion, intuition, logic, and practicality into account as you decide what to do.
- Breathe, relax, and take stock of your values. Then, make a choice and act on it.
- Trust yourself. You are wise, capable, and experienced. You know just what to do.

MEANINGS AND MESSAGES OF SEVEN OF VASES — REVERSED:

- Don't let your feelings overwhelm you. Feel, but also think clearly. Then act.
- Don't overthink this situation. Your intellect is important, but your intuition is too.

- You are pausing for too long to gather information and advice. You already have what you need to proceed.
- Swirl all aspects of yourself into the potion of your awareness as you formulate your next move. Don't value one trait (such as practicality or passion) over all others.
- Don't forget who you are, how you feel, and what you value. These are important keys to claiming the destiny that is yours.
- Stop telling yourself you are not qualified or prepared to make this choice. You are.

EIGHT OF VASES

TRANSFORM YOUR WORLD

GUIDANCE

Make a decision and you will open a portal. The time is right to leave one location or situation and move to another. You may feel unsettled by all the unknowns, but follow your inner knowing that sweeping change is essential for your growth.

In some life area, you have been feeling stagnant or stuck. Now, that is changing or is about to change. Even though you may feel worried or unsure, if you consult your intuition, you will tap into a strong inner certainty that you know just what to choose in order to bring about your beautiful next phase.

Don't hesitate. Don't wait until every little thing appears to line up perfectly. Commit to the change you crave without delay.

DYNAMICS

While there are moments in life when it is appropriate to rest, hang back, and regroup, this is not one of those times. Whether you've been deliberating for ages or have only recently begun to consider this present choice, the time to act is now. While it's true that there are many possibilities before you, you must say no to almost all of them now so you can say yes, decisively, to one.

Such choices can be challenging because in moving toward something, you move away from something else. Saying goodbye can be difficult, even in situations that are not ideal. The unknown can be frightening, and where you are is a known quantity in which you have managed to establish some degree of comfort. And you know in your heart of hearts that this is a point of no return. Even though you may physically be able to come back, the experience will never be the same.

The danger, now, is not in doing but in not doing. If you stay where you are, your spirit will be smothered and your mind will remain in a trap.

SECRETS

This scientist has been weighing and testing the liquid contents of her choices and has finally selected one over all the others. As she holds it to herself with decisive possessiveness, it begins the alchemical process of transforming her world. Its vapors bust through blocks and open a portal to infinity and infinite possibility.

She knows she has made the right decision, even as she makes peace with the fact that she can never go back to the way things were. She is saying goodbye to the old and hello to the new, with nostalgia for what was and happy anticipation for what is soon to be.

Even as a part of her dissolves, she knows she is making way for a new way of being to form.

MEANINGS AND MESSAGES OF EIGHT OF VASES:

- Leave an old situation so you can move into a new one.
- Follow your intuitive nudge to make a big life change.
- Be bold and set a sweeping change in motion, even though it contains a lot of unknowns.
- The time is right to make your move.
- Let go and let flow. Commit to change, trust the universe, and see what magic unfolds.

MEANINGS AND MESSAGES OF EIGHT OF VASES – REVERSED:

- Stop hanging on to an old and worn-out situation.
- Stop ignoring your intuitive nudge to make a big life change.
- You are waiting until all the conditions appear to be perfect, and it is keeping you stuck. Instead, make your move now and trust that everything will work out as it should.

- You feel drained because you are fighting the flow of the universe, which is unmistakably urging you to move on.
- You will feel a fresh rush of energy when you stop hanging on to conditions that are ready to go. Let go of what is tired and old so you can make room for all that is beautiful and new.

NINE OF VASES

A DREAM FULFILLED

GUIDANCE

You got what you wanted, and fulfillment is here (or is about to be). Experience pleasure and pride. Relax, breathe, and joyfully expand into this new status or stage.

You not only wished for something. You also envisioned, planned, and worked for it. And now it has arrived. It may be an inner condition, and it may be an outer one. Either way, in addition to providing you with immediate happiness, this condition places you in a position to earn greater material wealth and experience even more joy.

The manifestation of a dream is establishing the space for your dreamiest life conditions to continue to expand.

DYNAMICS

Some spiritual teachings would have us believe our emotions are separate from the physical things we want and the way we experience the material aspects of our lives, but this is not really the case.

While it is true that our status in the eyes of the world is merely a narrative or story, it's also true that our heart desires to live in a certain place and way, and to experience a specific type and degree of tangible affluence and success. Acting on your heart's desire allows you to build a meaningful life by interweaving your inner vision with your outer world.

Recognize your success. Feel the joy of inhabiting the tactile and three-dimensional destiny you have brought forth into form.

S E C R E T S

This goat saw a mountain and knew it was the one he wanted to climb. Some of his friends and family understood, and others did not quite, but none shared his exact vision for his future, for it was his destiny alone. And he followed it.

Now, at the top, he rests, and enjoys the view. He feels almost overcome with his great good fortune, even though he knows that through aligning his efforts and visions with divine power and orchestration, he played the largest role in bringing it into form.

He knows, too, that there will be other dreams and other challenges—other hills to climb—but for now, he takes pleasure in knowing that he set out to do something, and he did it. And in the process, he found a sense of accomplishment and delight.

The symbol for Venus indicates the presence of physical pleasure, emotional beauty, and lavish luxury.

MEANINGS AND MESSAGES OF NINE OF VASES:

- Acknowledge the wish that has been fulfilled and enjoy the accompanying feelings of pleasure and joy.
- Take joy in your lavish abundance and material success.
- A wish is about to be granted.
- Make a wish: the universe wants to grant it.
- Celebrate your victory and expand into your happiness.
- Take some time off after all your hard work.
- You climbed the mountain. Now relax and enjoy the view.

MEANINGS AND MESSAGES OF NINE OF VASES — REVERSED:

- A wish has been granted, but now you feel too overwhelmed to acknowledge and receive. Relax, breathe, and center your energy so you can enjoy all that you have.
- You may be feeling like your success is not deserved or is "too good to be true." Shift your beliefs to accommodate your good fortune and trust that it will not only last, but also expand.
- Relax your body and center your mind so you will be grounded and ready to receive.
- The universe wants to give you what you want, but first you must qualify and name it.
- Perform a solitary ritual or have a small get-together to celebrate and anchor in your success.

- If you don't stop for a moment to relax, you will miss an important opportunity to bring your goal to completion.
- Before you jump to the next phase, take some time to appreciate how far you've come.

TEN OF VASES

GRAND FINALE OF LOVE

GUIDANCE

Divine guidance communicated to you through your heart, and you followed it. Now, a beautiful conclusion is here. It is as if the universe holds you in starlight and the whole world showers you with love.

Take note of this grand finale of kindness, compassion, and nourishing support. Let it wash over you and saturate you. Feel it quench your endless thirst for love.

Gratitude is appropriate, but be sure to remember that you are a divine child, and you deserve blessings, adoration, and every wonderful thing. You deserve to love and be loved, to be surrounded by a loving community that supports you and wishes you all the best.

DYNAMICS

Life is an infinite continuum. Still, within the continuum, heart-centered narrative cycles play out, and their conclusive moments seem to shine especially brightly, like diamonds of sunlight on the surface of a lake. Obvious examples would be settling into your dream house, taking your newborn child home from the hospital, or marrying the love of your life. But there are less-flashy moments that can be equally profound, like watching the sunset with a partner, sharing a meal with a grown child, or laughing deeply with a friend.

Now is one of these times. Or whatever you are asking about holds the potential to be such a time.

S E C R E T S

The dark moon in the lower right corner is an ending. But a dark moon quickly becomes a new moon, so it is also a beginning.

Take joy in the conclusion of a cycle while joyfully expecting a happy new phase. Smile to what was, what is, and what shall be. Even the most glorious glimmer eventually shall fade away forever, so enjoy it as it lasts, while looking forward to the next glimmer that is already on its way.

Laurel grows out of two of the vases, symbolizing victory. Vases are emotion-centered, so this is a victory related to the heart. This correspondence is reinforced by the symbol for Venus in the bottom left corner — the planet of beauty and love.

MEANINGS AND MESSAGES OF TEN OF VASES:

- Heart-centered success is here.
- The happiest of all conclusions is happening or is on its way.
- A happy ending is also a beautiful beginning.
- Relax and enjoy the love you have called in.
- Domestic harmony has been achieved.
- Breathe, smile, celebrate, and let happiness wash over you.
- Appreciate the simple moments with your loved ones, as they are the most precious of all gifts.
- Expect a positive conclusion to this story.
- You have won, or will win, the emotional gold.

MEANINGS AND MESSAGES OF TEN OF VASES — REVERSED:

- You care so much about someone or something, it's currently overwhelming you.
- Ask for help from a professional or supportive family member or friend to help you regain your emotional bearings and find your way.
- A heartbreak or the end of an era may feel like the worst-case scenario, but it will increase your wisdom, deepen your capacity for joy, and clear the decks for a vital new phase.
- Don't let positive feelings overwhelm you or cause you to panic. Enjoy the good times while they last without clinging to them or worrying about the moment they will end.

- You may feel that your domestic harmony or your potential for domestic harmony is threatened. Instead of being hypervigilant, relax, invoke divine support, and seek clarity.
- All moments end, but then new ones begin. Practice enjoying the moment while it's here.
- Cultivate an appreciation for change and the passing of time.
- Embrace the mystery and surrender to uncertainty — even when you don't know what will happen, you can still trust that it will eventually turn out for the best.
- Welcome all your feelings and allow whatever happens to be.

PRINCESS OF VASES

DREAMY INITIATE

GUIDANCE

This princess is a young idealist or artist, or someone of any age who is embarking on a new journey of creativity or the heart. You may be about to receive important news about love, relationships, or emotions. Or, a sparkly-fresh wellspring of energy is flowing into your life from the watery realm of dreams.

Pay attention to your intuition. Follow your heart. Let your creativity and feelings flow. Identify where the Princess of Vases is showing up in this situation and take note of how she plays a part.

DYNAMICS

An idealistic initiate is all in. She has not seen or experienced enough to be world-weary or cynical, and she has no way of knowing precisely what she is signing up for.

While there is beauty and magic in this stage of the journey, there is also naivete. Expectations may be lofty or overly optimistic.

There is both danger and value in such a preliminary commitment to the dream. Jumping in with both feet, the Princess of Vases may sink, or she can quickly learn how to swim.

There is also a precious quality to the experience of starry-eyed excitement. Once we have passed through it, we can draw upon the memory of it, but we can never quite call it back again.

S E C R E T S

The Princess of Vases is wrapped in the pure white robe of the initiate. She is a maiden of the Goddess, and she is committed to her vow and her role. She gazes unblinkingly at the future, and she sees a perfect vision of the peaceful and loving world she intends to create.

Dipping her hand holy water, she prepares to baptize a beautiful new condition, and to call forth its loftiest expression and all its potential for love.

A leaf from the laurel vine that grows from the vase covers one eye, as her youthful belief in the possibility for perfection obscures her ability to see the more nuanced truth.

At the same time, beginner's luck and the protective and auspicious energy of laurel lend an irrepressible boost of success.

MEANINGS AND MESSAGES OF PRINCESS OF VASES:

- A young or youthful idealist has appeared in this situation.
- You are embarking on a new creative project or endeavor of the heart.
- Expect news about creativity, passion, or love.
- Intuition is flowing, and new avenues of psychic vision are opening up.
- You are dazzled by a new possibility or project.
- A romantic notion has captured your imagination.
- You are in the initial stages of romantic love.
- You are being initiated into an exclusive organization or friend group.
- You are an initiate of something fresh and new that centers on intuition, creativity, spirituality, or the heart.

MEANINGS AND MESSAGES OF PRINCESS OF VASES — REVERSED:

- A formerly idealistic person, now jaded, has something to do with this situation. (This might be you.)
- A creative project or endeavor of the heart is not what you thought it was, and you've lost enthusiasm.
- News about creativity, passion, or love is delayed or not what you hoped it would be.
- Stop ignoring your intuition — pay attention to your psychic visions and nudges.

- The reality of a possibility or project brings disillusionment and the need to reformulate your opinion and approach.
- After being carried away by a romantic notion, reality is setting in. But that doesn't have to be a negative — it might simply be helpful information that requires a different tactic.
- You are beginning to see someone for who they are instead of how they initially appeared.
- You have uncovered a codependent or cult-like dynamic.
- A person, group, or situation is not what you initially believed. Get clear and choose the next steps accordingly.

KNIGHT OF VASES

ROMANTIC CHAMPION

GUIDANCE

This is an amorous person in their 20s or 30s or a romantic dreamer of any age. Deep emotions are flowing and aching to be expressed. Connect with your feelings so you can fluidly declare them and let them be known.

Life is beautiful and love is the magic ingredient that brings your heart to life. Open to love and be willing to be vulnerable. Enjoy the dreamy transcendence of romance and romantic love.

Whether the Knight of Vases signifies you or someone else, be aware of their presence in this situation and the ethereal love potion they swirl into the mix.

DYNAMICS

The Knight of Vases is the essence of romantic poetry and love songs.

If this card signifies a person, they wish to communicate their ardent feelings and are deeply enamored of something or someone (maybe you).

The Knight of Vases is connected to their heart and filled to the brim with feelings. Their ideal is born from emotion, and it moves them forward on a wellspring and wave of passionate love.

Even though they are in the initial stages of love—which are famously idealistic and not entirely clear-eyed—their aim is true. They want to be known, seen, and appreciated, and to appreciate deeply in return.

SECRETS

The Knight of Vases speaks words of love, which is why the symbol for Venus lies at their throat.

In addition to speaking words of love, their ears ache to hear them.

The crescent moon at their brow signifies their watery wisdom and clairvoyance, which are not objective, but influenced by their wishes and passionate love.

Rays flow behind them from the base of their skull, the energy center known as the Mouth of God chakra, which channels high vibratory messages from the Divine.

Even though romance is always laced with illusion, it can also be a channel of the purest wisdom.

Enjoy the fantasy, but consciously connect with the highest level of truth.

MEANINGS AND MESSAGES OF KNIGHT OF VASES:

- A romantic dreamer in their 20s or 30s, or an amorous suitor of any age, has appeared in this situation.
- You or someone else has deep feelings that want to be expressed.
- Write a poem or song about your feelings or speak words of love from your heart.
- Allow someone else the time and space to express their feelings to you.
- Open your heart to love.
- Allow yourself to get carried away by the joy of romance and the early stages of romantic love, but also enlist divine wisdom and align with truth.
- Prioritize romance.

MEANINGS AND MESSAGES OF KNIGHT OF VASES – REVERSED:

- Someone in this situation (maybe you) is obsessing over someone, letting their emotions get carried away by illusion, or displaying stalker-like tendencies.

- Your feelings are obscuring the truth. Get your bearings and look more honestly at the situation before you express yourself or proceed.
- Even though love poetry or songs written in your honor may be dazzling, postpone judgment until the composer's true nature is revealed.
- Don't dance around the truth. Speak from your heart, but also say what you mean plainly, and encourage others to do the same.
- Don't just open your heart to the idea of love, but to actual love, which encompasses not just the divine perfection of another person, but also their temporary foibles and faults.
- Be patient with the process of getting to know someone on all levels. Don't hold them to impossible standards, but don't overlook problems or be overly permissive either.
- Let yourself enjoy romance, but don't forget that it is always a bit of an illusion. While new love feels euphoric and elevated, lasting love contains ups, downs, and boring in-betweens.

QUEEN OF VASES

INTUITIVE NURTURER

GUIDANCE

This is a sensitive and compassionate person at middle age or older, or a wise and intuitive nurturer of any age. Employ your psychic abilities and creative gifts. Spirituality and healing are of the essence.

Tune in to the lush and nourishing current of dreams and heart-centered employment. Meditate, relax, revel in your senses, do something you love, or just be. Float happily in the ocean of spiritual bliss.

Perhaps you need to lean on a gentle and comforting parental figure right now, or it could be that you will do well to be the maternal person who offers love and support to another being or group.

DYNAMICS

The Queen of Vases is relaxed and fluid, physically present and open, while mentally and emotionally at one with the realm of spirituality, emotion, poetry, and dreams.

Her beauty transcends time and space, as she is a channel of cosmic healing and the wisdom of the ages.

Emotions contain the full spectrum, and the breadth of one's true happiness directly correlates with the depth of their pain. The Queen of Vases, however, is adept at keeping her heart open, for she knows that feeling her feelings is what taps her into her endless wellspring of joy.

Indeed, the Queen of Vases equally welcomes both nostalgia and pleasure, heartache and hearty delight.

Her creativity is not separate from her, and her spiritual insight shows her all she needs to know.

S E C R E T S

The Queen of Vases is a mermaid with a double tail, which is an affirmation of her openness, fertility, and sensual freedom.

The symbol of Venus and femininity hovers above her.

Along the circle, the Eye of Providence illustrates her deep intuition, which perpetually guides her to surrender to, and align with, the natural flow of life.

Rubedo, the ruby red elixir of creation, enters the crown of her head from her literal golden crown.

As she opens her heart, the water of life drips from her nipple. Although the water of life is infinite, as it enters the portal of existence, it transforms into *albedo*, the white fluid of death and mortality. Then, just as quickly, the albedo enters the ocean of everything, and the cycle of life is renewed.

MEANINGS AND MESSAGES OF QUEEN OF VASES:

- A mature and queenlike nurturer has appeared in this situation.
- Employ or cultivate your psychic abilities.
- Take joy in creating and expressing.
- Heal yourself or another, or seek out the healing you need.
- Find the current of joy and let it carry you forward.
- Do what you love and get into a zone.
- Be a loving nurturer for yourself or someone else.
- The natural flow of life is propelling you along its current.
- Seek out or receive support from a compassionate parental figure.
- Relax, calm your mind, and let your feelings flow.

MEANINGS AND MESSAGES OF QUEEN OF VASES — REVERSED:

- A mature person, or a person of any age (maybe you), is being emotionally manipulative or is getting carried away by their emotions.
- Question what seems like an intuitive nudge. Fear, assumption, hope, or expectation may be posing as inner knowing.
- Cultivate good habits and create the space for success. For success and sustainability, artistic expression needs practical guidelines and structure.
- Revisit and revise a healing strategy.

- Examine addictive behaviors and heal patterns of excess, codependency, or abuse.
- Obsession is distracting you from joy and contributing to patterns of imbalance.
- Love and nurture without seeking to control.
- Tune in to your intuition and surrender to the flow of life.
- A parental figure or seemingly helpful friend may be manipulating you or using your feelings against you.
- You are temporarily agitated or overwhelmed. Relax and take some downtime to recharge.

KING OF VASES
LEVIATHAN OF LOVE

GUIDANCE

The King of Vases is an astute and heart-centered person, middle age or older, or an intuitive, creative, and empathetic adept of any age. Surrender your ego to the part of you that is one with everything so you may transcend false stories and see through the eyes of the heart. Let emotional intelligence take over.

The answer is love. Flood yourself with love and let that love extend to those around you. Look deeply, and you will see that everyone's motivation is either love or a desire for more love.

You can lead with compassion, repair broken lines of communication, and shift dynamics for the better when you follow the way of the King of Vases and generously channel the healing elixir of love.

DYNAMICS

While human motivations may sometimes seem straightforward, there is always a sea of dreams, memories, and emotions that lies under the surface. We may believe we can carry our feelings in a single vase, containing and keeping them small, but this is never true.

The King of Vases knows that he must surrender, again and again, to the truth of who he is: an ancient sage who resides in and is synonymous with the depths of the sea.

You will benefit from following his example and surrendering your human expectations and machinations for the majestic and formidable part of you perpetually immersed in spirit, feeling, and the vast unknown.

SECRETS

Did you think the King of Vases was the little man falling from the sky? No. That is only how he temporarily appears, at times. His true self is the whale.

When the whale swallows the man, the man will return to the completeness of his being.

In much the same way that a vase holds the very same water that comprises the ocean, you hold the very same spirit that is everywhere and in everything. The secret is that your human identity is not the vase, but the universal water of Spirit it contains. When you remember this truth, you can be both the vase and the ocean: both the human and the incredible depths of poetry, magic, symbolism, dreams, and the sacred saltwater of human tears.

The vase falls with the man, just as the crown has tumbled from his head. He wears not a velvet gown, but long underwear, for he has been stripped of the illusions of human importance so he can merge with the eternal and the vast.

The symbol of Venus indicates the prevalence and potency of love.

MEANINGS AND MESSAGES OF KING OF VASES:

- A wise, compassionate, and mature person has appeared in this situation.
- Love is of the essence: look for the love and magnify it.
- Love yourself and extend that love to others.
- Connect with dreams, poetry, magic, and intuition.
- Let your feelings flow.
- Lead or provide for others from a heart-centered place.
- Consult your heart and let it lead you.

MEANINGS AND MESSAGES OF KING OF VASES — REVERSED:

- Someone in this situation (it could be you) is behaving in an emotionally immature way.
- Release jealous and petty behavior.

- Don't seek to hoard all the love for yourself — love is a vast and endless sea. It is not a finite resource.
- Look for ways to offer yourself more unconditional approval and generous self-care. Once you end the inner drought, offer love to others and see what they are doing through eyes of love. Then proceed.
- Stop ignoring your intuition and desire to express yourself creatively.
- Connect with your feelings.
- Recalibrate your motivations so you can tend to your day-to-day concerns with presence and love.
- Stop making choices from your ego. Stop ignoring your heart.

ACE OF WANDS

SPARK TO FLAME

GUIDANCE

A spark is becoming a fire. The sun is rising on a positive new condition. You can trust what you are asking about or experiencing, as the radiant light of good fortune is shining on you.

Luck is on your side. You are blowing on the embers of your destiny. The spark of your hopes will catch, grow, and become a glorious flame.

Things are moving, and quickly. You have conceived something fabulous and are now setting it into motion, such as a creative project, an adventure, a relationship, a big life change, or even a child.

Be daring and show up. Let your light shine. Don't hide who you are or talk yourself out of your dreams.

DYNAMICS

Ace of Wands is the purest expression of the fire element — the spark, the flame, and the inferno. To the alchemist, it's the lead at the very instant it is transformed into the living essence of gold.

If you've ever waited for the sunrise and then been struck by the magic of the sun's blinding luminosity as it first peeks above the horizon, you have directly encountered the energy of the Ace of Wands. It is the innocent purity of fire and the refreshing power of early morning light.

Hope is here. There is much to happily anticipate. Anything is possible, and the powers that be are on your side. You are solar-powered. Your fire of fortune is stoked. Your luck is radiant, inexhaustible, and divinely ordained.

SECRETS

The symbol for fire is in the upper right corner, and the larger triangle contains the feathers of angel wings: divine favor ushering you toward your most positive outcome.

The symbol for lead is hovering near the tip of the fiery wand. What is heavy and inert has transformed into a dancing flame.

The sun rises near the symbol for the wee hours of the morning, when the sun is still hiding beneath the horizon, but the light of possibility slowly begins to light up the sky, heralding hope and the return of the dawn.

The salamander is a magical creature of fire: a living flame of passion, expansiveness, and optimism. Above his head is a dry leaf, ready to be ignited by the spark of his intention, which will expand to fill the sky with light.

Like the sun itself, the flame of the sword lights up the waxing moon, creating a resonance of freshness and new possibility.

MEANINGS AND MESSAGES OF ACE OF WANDS:

- Be optimistic. The light of luck is shining on you.
- You have much to happily anticipate. Take guided action, and you will succeed.
- The sun is rising. Positive new conditions are dawning or are just about to dawn.
- Energy is moving, and good things are happening.
- This is an affirmative. Proceed with what you are considering.
- Your inspiration is stoked. You are creating something beautiful.
- A new relationship or a happy life change is on the horizon.

MEANINGS AND MESSAGES OF ACE OF WANDS — REVERSED:

- Rise up out of negativity and worry so the light of luck can shine on you.

- Don't procrastinate for one moment more. Act now to activate the good fortune that is yours to claim.
- Step out of your comfort zone to experience success.
- When you believe that whatever happens is ultimately for your highest good, you will indeed find that to be the case.
- Finally accept your intuitive hits and act on them, so you can let the light of your destiny shine.
- Denying your creative impulses is making you feel depressed or physically unwell. Embrace them instead to turn this dynamic around.
- Get clear on your intentions and your fondest desires. Then act, and trust that everything is working out for you — and it will.

TWO OF WANDS

A FIRE WILL BURN

GUIDANCE

A creative vision or plans for a new endeavor are coming together. You have identified and gathered the materials you need to build a dazzling firework of success. Celebrate, for you are stoking the fire of a beautiful new condition.

This is a dynamic, flammable time where the sparks of your desire can quickly begin to turn into an inferno. Be clear on what you desire and be ready to act quickly to bring it into physical form. Consciously relax your body and mind so you don't get overwhelmed by the speed with which things might begin to happen. It is best to be clear-headed, so you will be poised to jump masterfully into the action.

You may be surprised by just how rapidly and successfully things transform. So, expand into possibility rather than contracting out of fear. Expect and welcome in an even grander outcome than you formerly could have foreseen.

DYNAMICS

Two of Wands is the vibrant duality of fire: a match to a matchbox or two sticks struck together to build a flame.

By assembling and calling in the conditions and ideas you need, you have arranged your dry kindling in such a way that you need only apply your fiery vision and it will erupt into a dancing interplay of heat, light, and sparks that reach toward the sky.

This is a moment of both choice and potential. Be very clear on what you want and be ready for your success to grow at a speed and volume that far exceed what you previously had in mind.

SECRETS

Near the tips of the flaming wands, we see the symbol for lead, the heavy metal that becomes transformed into alchemical gold. In the upper right corner, we see the symbol for the fire element.

Two of Wands is a reminder that you are more powerful and loved than you suspect. When you work magic for manifestation through intention, visualization, and other forms of inner alchemy, the universe wants to show off for you, not just by meeting but by far exceeding your expectations for what is possible.

Two of Wands says: your life can be filled with miracles, magic, and joy. As you continue to push the boundaries of your visions and manifested goals, your life will be your Great Work, where you interweave your human consciousness with divine consciousness and endlessly bring your heart's innermost desires into external form, for the highest and truest good of all.

MEANINGS AND MESSAGES OF TWO OF WANDS:

- You have what you need to succeed.
- Be clear on what you want, as this is a time of rapid manifestation.
- Expand your vision of what is possible.
- Invoke divine support and allow it to exceed your expectations.
- Take action on a creative project or goal.
- Celebrate, for you are poised to do and create precisely what you most desire.
- You have positioned yourself perfectly, and now a fabulous opportunity is here.

MEANINGS AND MESSAGES OF TWO OF WANDS – REVERSED:

- You have what you need to succeed, but you have to take a chance on it.
- The universe wants to give you what you want, but first, you must get clear on what, exactly, that is.

- Don't settle, stay small, or play it safe. Open up to what you really want and go for it.
- Remember to ask the Divine for help and revise any limiting beliefs holding you back.
- Don't procrastinate for one moment more.
- Sometimes what we most fear is tied to what we most desire. Overcome the fear so you can go for what you want.
- An opportunity is here for you, but you must allow yourself to see it.

THREE OF WANDS

THE FIRE IS STOKED

GUIDANCE

The momentum has been set in motion — let it carry you forward, and be willing to go where it takes you. Let inspiration inform your actions and encourage your joy. Make the brave decisions that feed your passion and stoke the fire at your heart.

This is a time to expand, move forward, and bust out of your comfort zone in daring leaps and bounds. Your mind may try to talk you out of what your soul knows by presenting you with all the reasons you shouldn't or can't do what you would most like to do. But life gets stale when we obey our inner naysayer. Instead, obey your inner warrior.

The journey has already begun, so don't stop now. Even if you end up somewhere totally different than where you expected, it will be somewhere remarkable indeed — possibly even better and more beautiful than you previously foresaw.

DYNAMICS

The friction of two wands has given birth to a third entity: a spark that is quickly becoming a flame, which in turn becomes fuel for forward movement.

If you feel obsessed or fixated on an idea or plan, don't discount that thought or try to talk yourself out of it. There is a reason for it. Let it guide you. Honor it, map it out, and look for opportunities to follow where it leads.

There is danger here, but it is not in acting — it is in staying still or boxing yourself in. For an inner fire is a precious, sentient thing. Like all living things, if it is deprived of oxygen, it will die.

SECRETS

Two wands have given birth to a third, which is also a vehicle: a sacred river raft cradled by the moon and air currents, and navigated by a little man in a red cap.

That little man is you, letting yourself be carried by Spirit while simultaneously making your own way.

The red cap symbolizes *amanita muscaria* — the magic mushroom that obliterates the ego and the imaginary barriers between heart and mind, body and spirit.

In the lower right, we see the symbol for Saturn and lead.

Saturn is the planet of consolidation and focus. Your talents have been honed, and your mastery in a certain area has brought you to this point.

Lead, to the alchemists, contains everything you need to create gold. It simply awaits the alchemist's great work. That work is comprised of your brave, inspired, and divinely guided action.

MEANINGS AND MESSAGES OF THREE OF WANDS:

- The journey has already begun. Merge with the magic you've set in motion and let its momentum carry you forward.
- Pay attention to your inner nudges and act on your intuition — the universe is conspiring to help you and move you along.
- Things will unfold quickly and miraculously if you bravely act on your goals.
- A seeming setback is, in truth, a blessing. Believe that everything is working in your favor, and it will.
- Opportunities are everywhere for you, propelling you forward into glorious success. Go with them and flow with them.
- This is an energetic upgrade. It will demand quick and courageous action, so jump into the flow of things and be willing to take calculated risks.

MEANINGS AND MESSAGES OF THREE OF WANDS — REVERSED:

- Stop questioning what you know in your heart feels right.
- Don't stay where you are out of fear. Don't try to talk yourself out of your goals. Flow with the universe and let Spirit lead the way.
- You will unlock a divine momentum when you take a risk and take bold action on your own behalf.
- A setback will be a setback, *unless* you are willing to entertain the possibility that it is actually a blessing in disguise.
- Even though you have been willfully ignoring opportunities, it's not too late. Another one will present itself shortly or is presenting itself now. Act on it without delay and you will merge with divine momentum and flow.
- Don't let the fear of disappointment dissuade you from going for what you want. The only way to ensure failure is to never let yourself try.

FOUR OF WANDS

FOUR OF WANDS

PAUSE TO CELEBRATE

GUIDANCE

A goal has been reached, and a cycle has been completed. Now, step back, observe the big picture, and attune to the eternal perfection that underlies the ups and downs of this life experience. Celebrate a rite of passage or a big and happy change.

Something you have long desired is coming to you or has recently made itself at home in your life. A relationship has matured or moved into a new phase of commitment, you have upgraded to a beautiful new living arrangement, or you have reached another milestone in your family, friend group, business, self-growth, career, education, or finances.

Take a moment to observe this victory in a public way. Don't just keep working. Make plans for a party. Send out announcements. Perform a ritual or observance of some kind with others, such as a graduation party or wedding reception. Or simply take a group of loved ones out for dinner or drinks.

D Y N A M I C S

Life is an endless journey and a ceaseless flow of change. Still, there are moments when you get to rejoice, breathe, and expand into a feeling of contentment with all that you are and all that you have.

While on one level, it may seem like celebrations and observances are useless luxuries that only serve to distract, they are in fact a vital key to helping you process, metabolize, and enjoy positive change. Think of exhaling before you inhale or taking some time off so you can recalibrate and be at your best. Similarly, celebration helps you savor the sweetness of life and soak in its nourishment. Celebration isn't just a casual bonus, but a vital prerequisite of a life well lived.

S E C R E T S

This earthly couple embodies the divine polarities of pure potentiality and the fire of passion and sensual life. Their union is both earthly and sacred, tangible and transcendent. In its daily friction, it generates spiritual illumination. In its imperfection, it is perfect. This is why they have decided to celebrate: to announce their wedding and share their joy with the world.

The symbol for lead and Saturn hovers above the woman's right shoulder. To the alchemists, lead contains everything needed to create gold. Saturn is the planet of limitation, and commitment is a positive limitation. For example, in a marriage vow, by saying yes to one thing, you say no to all others. This creates a container for trust, which facilitates joy, collaboration, and personal growth.

MEANINGS AND MESSAGES OF FOUR OF WANDS:

- You have succeeded at a goal and are graduating to a new level of success.
- Throw a party or arrange a gathering to celebrate a blessing or breakthrough.
- Acknowledge the subtle or obvious milestone you have reached.
- Expect something wonderful to happen. Then, be sure to share the news and take some time to observe it according to its due.

MEANINGS AND MESSAGES OF FOUR OF WANDS — REVERSED:

- Something is keeping you from succeeding at a goal or graduating to a new level of success. Once you acknowledge this roadblock, you can easily remove it and move forward according to your desires.
- Stop and take time to celebrate your blessing or breakthrough, or make plans to do so soon. Don't let the joyful moments of your life pass you by.

- It's not too late to acknowledge a milestone. Even if it's belated, look deeply at what you've achieved and share your joy with your loved ones.
- Something wonderful has happened or is about to happen, but you aren't seeing it. Look closely, name it, celebrate it, and let yourself delight in your happiness and luck.

FIVE OF WANDS

FIVE OF WANDS

CONSTRUCTIVE CONFLICT

G U I D A N C E

You have encountered a challenge — rise to it. Collaborate, compete, and stoke the fires of your passion and sense of adventure. Believe in yourself because you have everything you need to succeed.

Constructive conflict—a healthy mix of opposing factions, objectives, and perspectives—will bring about a high-quality product or fabulous outcome.

Be willing to undergo temporary friction, hassle, and uncertainty to reach a new level of mastery or attain a much-cherished goal.

At the same time, prioritize kindness. Respect all perspectives. Stand up for yourself and say what you need to say, but don't hesitate to apologize if you accidentally hurt someone's feelings or say something you regret.

DYNAMICS

Life will present you with trials: enormous, tiny, and everywhere in between. A mindset of avoidance will not serve you. A sporting mindset will. Assume that whatever happens is intriguing and fun and will ultimately benefit you in some significant way. Approach each battle or obstacle with playfulness, curiosity, and confidence in your ability to prevail.

Disciplines such as martial arts, debate, business, and competitive sports all employ the refining sparks of conflict for the sake of personal evolution, professional improvement, accomplishment, and satisfying play. This is the wisdom of the Five of Wands in action, which can be applied to anything that seems to be an obstacle or problem.

Where interpersonal relationships are concerned, look beyond the surface levels of discord to see the positive regard that underlies them. Remember that we usually don't get too bent out of shape by someone's words or actions unless it's someone we like and appreciate or, at the very least, respect.

SECRETS

The human hand is a miraculous feature of personal mastery and skill. The right hand, specifically, is an appendage of action — of dynamic accomplishment and deliberate change. The five fiery wands hovering at each fingertip multiply the ambition and dynamism at work.

In the upper right corner, we see the symbol for the fire element.

In the lower left corner is the symbol for lead, which contains all the alchemical ingredients to make gold.

Behind the hand is the ultimate representation of fire, action, and spiritual gold: the sun.

So, if the sun is behind the hand, what light is casting the shadow from in front of it? It is the courage that burns eternally at your very own heart, which, indeed, is even brighter and more powerful than the sun.

Gaze at your palm as it is depicted here. Contemplate the fiery swords hovering above it. And consider the immense power that is at your fingertips now.

MEANINGS AND MESSAGES OF FIVE OF WANDS:

- Rise to this challenge with a sense of adventure, and you will succeed.
- Let conflict or conflicting perspectives spark and feed the fires of creativity.
- Friction is stoking positive change.
- The effort you are expending is moving you forward.
- Speak your truth and stand up for yourself with respect for your shared objectives and for everyone concerned.
- Respectfully fight for your principles and visions while also being willing to compromise and to see things from fresh and diverse points of view.

MEANINGS AND MESSAGES OF FIVE OF WANDS — REVERSED:

- Don't dissemble — face this challenge head-on.
- Don't seek to avoid conflict.
- Be patient with the process of discussing and hashing out the details with your partners, collaborators, or teammates.
- Now is not the time to be passive or take a break.
- Cooperate proactively. Resist the urge to act from meanness, or to resort to underhanded tactics to get your way.
- Be receptive to other ways of seeing and doing things while also swirling your unique perspectives and abilities into the mix.

SIX OF WANDS
VICTORY DANCE

GUIDANCE

You have won, are winning, or are about to win. You've worked hard and stayed the course, and now all your effort is paying off. Celebrate your victory and plan some well-deserved time off.

If you haven't quite reached the finish line, you're almost there. Keep going.

If you *have* reached the finish line, behold the good fortune before you, and let yourself admit: you did this. Yes, there were other factors involved, but without consistently acting on your vision, even while facing struggles and setbacks, you would not be in this coveted position. Without utilizing your strengths and acting on your wisdom, you would not have cause for this victory dance.

Take a deep breath. Smile. It was a long way to the top, but you made it. Tomorrow, you can formulate a new strategy and plan for what to do next. But today (or in the days ahead), give yourself a break. Appreciate all your hard work. And celebrate.

DYNAMICS

Every worthwhile endeavor contains ups and downs. Similarly, within the larger battle, there are smaller ones, some of which you win and some of which you inevitably lose. Congratulate yourself, as none of your losses dissuaded you from keeping your eye on the finish line. And now you have succeeded (or are about to succeed) at your goal.

Even though life is an endlessly spiraling journey and a kaleidoscopic mandala of light, it's also true that a particular story cycle of your life is becoming complete. When you relax and joyfully acknowledge this conclusion, you will metabolize your success and consolidate your accomplishments, which will, in turn, prepare you for the next swirling cycle in your quest.

SECRETS

Amidst six victorious wands, we see the symbol for lead, and above that the symbol for gold and then the symbol for the waxing moon. The hard work of the alchemist paid off: lead became gold, and now that gold is continuing to rise and expand.

Above these symbols, we see a warrior performing an impromptu victory dance, as a glorious crown hovers above her head.

Her left nipple is an open eye, symbolizing her receptive perception, the wisdom that lives in her body, and her willingness to nourish the world with her awakened vision.

She dances in front of the sun, recharging, as a larger waxing moon hovers beneath her open hand.

In her posture, we see both celebration and exhaustion. She has worked hard, and she knows it. Now, she is letting her tension dissipate as the sweetness of conscious victory moves through her body in the form of music and dance. This heals and recalibrates her energy before she sleeps deeply and wakes to embark on her next beautiful challenge and glorious new phase.

MEANINGS AND MESSAGES OF SIX OF WANDS:

- You are succeeding or are about to succeed.
- Be sure to relax and celebrate after your victory.
- Acknowledge what you've accomplished and how hard you've worked.
- It wasn't easy, but you did it. Congratulations.
- Throw a party to celebrate your success, and then take at least a day or two off to recharge.

MEANINGS AND MESSAGES OF SIX OF WANDS — REVERSED:

- Success is here for you, but you must look for it and expect it before it will be visible.
- Hang in there, and don't give up yet.

- If you don't take time to celebrate and acknowledge your victory, you will feel drained and miss out on the sweetness of life.
- You are temporarily blinded by your setbacks and are failing to see that the overall outcome is, or can be, success.
- You've been going too hard for too long, and it's wearing on you. Look for all your successes and celebrate them. Then, take some time to recharge.

SEVEN OF WANDS

THE WOLF MOTHER IS AWAKE

GUIDANCE

Defend what is vital. Protect your energy, banish intruders, and set boundaries around your time. Summon your courage to stand up for yourself, your loved ones, and your values.

After reaching a goal or establishing a condition you care about, or any time you harbor love for a person or passion for a particular cause, you inherit the responsibility to preserve and defend that which is precious to you.

Sometimes the requirement for such fierce protectiveness will feel like a burden. But even when it seems to drain you and to require an exorbitant amount of your attention and time, remember that caring about something so dearly is what makes life worthwhile.

At the same time, if you reach a breaking point, you may need to ask for help, reexamine your values, or revisit the way you budget your time. Take care of yourself appropriately so you can effectively protect your treasure and your turf.

DYNAMICS

After the arduous task of giving birth to pups, a wolf mother barely has time to recoup before she steps into her role as defender, provider, and guide. Her job feels all-encompassing, yet she wouldn't trade it.

If she believes her pups may be threatened in any way, even by a predator who is larger or faster than she is, she will put her life on the line to defend them without the slightest hesitation.

Seven of Wands is Mars in Leo: worldly success and personal victory as the result of a hard-won fight. Only, as perhaps you are now realizing, the battle is never over: now that you have obtained what you want, if you want to keep it, you must defend it and nurture it so you can help it to thrive.

SECRETS

Wolf mother magic is absolute love, meticulous care, and fiery protection, swirled into one. The wolf reminds you that you must summon your energy reserves on behalf of these aims. At the same time, you must be careful not to burn yourself out, so you can show up again at this task. Remember that wolves are pack animals: they don't hesitate to accept help and protection from other members of their family and community. Ask for help if you need it.

The symbol for lead in this image indicates that your alchemical work is not finished: you must diligently continue the great work of transforming the base metals of the mundane world into spiritual gold.

MEANINGS AND MESSAGES OF SEVEN OF WANDS:

- Protect your loved ones and your home turf.
- Consistently and conscientiously nurture a career, condition, or cause.
- Defend what you care about.
- Take care of yourself and recharge your personal energy so you can continue the great work to which you are called. Perhaps ask friends or family for help.
- Your hard work has brought you success, but don't mistake this for a reason to rest on your laurels. Sometimes, success demands even harder and more persistent work. This is most certainly one of those times.

MEANINGS AND MESSAGES OF SEVEN OF WANDS — REVERSED:

- You are feeling unhinged or out of sorts in response to a perceived threat to you, your loved ones, or your home. Take a moment to breathe, relax your body, and center your mind. Plan a logical and efficient defense. Then proceed.
- Don't be inconsistent or irresponsible, or you may lose that which you have worked so hard to create.
- Trust that you are qualified to defend that which you care about.

- You have burned yourself out and now you are out of balance. Rest, eat healthy food, drink plenty of water, and then get right back in the game.
- You've been going it alone, but help is here for you. Ask for it.
- You thought that once you reached your goal, everything would be easy, breezy, and fun, but you are now learning that is not the case. Accept this, and step into your new role, along with all the responsibility it requires.

EIGHT OF WANDS

BREAKTHROUGH

GUIDANCE

The time for deliberation is over. Act decisively and get things moving. Break through barriers and demolish delays.

Things may have seemed sluggish and stuck, but all that is over now. Something has shifted, or is about to shift, so everything can finally fly forward at full speed. Dive into the fast pace that is already in motion, and it will propel you into success.

Start where you are and do what you can with what you have. The next steps will soon be revealed. Your inner fire will fuel your action and light your way.

DYNAMICS

All tasks seem harder and less possible before you simply begin. Even chores that seem onerous or unmanageable can often become fun once you transcend your hesitation and get started. But don't worry so much about where to start — just start somewhere, and then continue.

Get into a flow, and the universe will fire up your engine, activate help from seen and unseen worlds, and begin to carry you along at a rapid velocity.

When the fire of divine change is burning, you might as well stoke the flames. You can try, but you can't hang on to the way things were. In addition to being disappointed, you will also miss out on all the many blessings that the fire of transformation will bring.

You can't stop change, but you can frame it in any way you choose, and whatever you choose will be true for you. You can see it as a tragedy or a blessing, an abomination or an opportunity, an obstacle or a boon. Choose a narrative that helps you rather than harms you and channel the fiery friction of change toward a sparkling inferno of positivity, clarity, and light.

S E C R E T S

First, there was the appearance of a pile of sticks. Then, an ax came out of nowhere and cut one of them in half. Then, instantly, each stick revealed itself to be a fiery wand, flying in one direction or another, and opening a portal to infinity, and to joy.

The symbol for lead illustrates that this situation already contains all that is needed to create spiritual gold. The glowing suns and fiery wands indicate the dynamic transformation that is happening even as we speak.

The ax is a blunt instrument, but it is effective. And this one comes from Spirit. Spirit is telling you to give stagnation the ax.

Grab that blade, pick a roadblock (any roadblock), and give it a whack. Then, keep chopping away.

Don't let anything stop or delay you. If anything appears to be in the way, break it in half.

MEANINGS AND MESSAGES OF EIGHT OF WANDS:

- Glorious momentum is finally here.
- Get fired up and flow with positive change.
- The time to act is now.
- Spirit is moving you forward.
- This is the breakthrough you've been waiting for.
- These changes are for the best. Welcome them.
- Look for opportunities, and you will find them.
- It doesn't matter where you begin — just start. Then continue.

MEANINGS AND MESSAGES OF EIGHT OF WANDS — REVERSED:

- Don't worry so much about where to start; just start.
- If you resist or ignore it, positive change will pass you by.
- Don't hesitate for one moment more.
- Uncomfortable conditions are Spirit's way of getting you moving.
- Rapid change is happening whether you like it or not, so you may as well make friends with it and let it carry you forward.

- Stop fighting this change and look for the blessings and possible blessings it contains.
- Expect roadblocks, and you will find them. Look for opportunities instead.
- Perfectionism and worry are holding you back. Stop hesitating — just start anywhere and then continue.

NINE OF WANDS
CRITICAL POINT

GUIDANCE

Furious or prolonged effort has left you feeling drained and vulnerable. The birth or rebirth you have been working toward is coming. But more work is still necessary to bring it forth.

As out of reach as it may seem, seek the most helpful balance between shoring up your energy and powering through. While you can't stop now if you want to achieve your goal or bring about the ideal conclusion to a vital narrative arc, you are also almost at your limit, and you need to recharge.

Pay attention to boundaries. Get rest when possible. Take care of yourself as best you can. But don't call it a day just yet.

Be wary of intruders and those who would take advantage of your battle-weariness and the temporary weakness that goes along with bringing forth something vulnerable and new.

Stubbornly fight for what you care about for just one more battle or a few moments more.

DYNAMICS

In some ways, you are like a mother fox about to give birth to her cub. In other ways, you are the cub. Indeed, you are both: the life giver and the one who is born.

You may be bringing forth a new life phase, a new degree of wisdom, a creative project of some kind.

This baby fox, if she survives her youth, will grow up to be like her mother: fiery, wily, and wise. Together, they can support each other, protect each other, and shore up the other's joy.

But in this moment, both baby and mother are exhausted from the important work of the birthing process. While this is a natural side effect of the process, it is also one more thing to watch out for. In addition to everything else, they must compensate for the temporary depletion of their defenses.

SECRETS

This baby fox is in a magician's crucible. Mastery is required. The alchemical fire that will strengthen the cub may also kill her.

Be bold but delicate. Pay attention to your needs, but also draw on your energy reserves. You can establish the conditions you desire, but you must incorporate all your strength, along with focus, diligence, and mindful self-care.

This is the great work. You are bringing forth spiritual gold.

MEANINGS AND MESSAGES OF NINE OF WANDS:

- You have pushed it to the limit, but you're not finished. Keep going.
- Take care of yourself, but also work hard and push through.
- Something beautiful is about to be born: keep focusing and doing your best.
- Compensate for the vulnerabilities that come from prolonged focus and hard work.
- Protect your energy and boundaries so you can bring a project or goal to completion.
- Find the balance between shoring up your energy and expending energy as needed.
- Keep at it! You're almost there.

MEANINGS AND MESSAGES OF NINE OF WANDS — REVERSED:

- You are in danger of giving up just before success is achieved. Regain your balance and push through.
- Take care of yourself *and* work hard. It doesn't have to be one or the other. Do your best to find a balance that works.
- You may think you're finished and it's time to celebrate, but you're not there yet. Keep at it and keep your guard up.
- You're exhausted because you've been working toward a cherished goal. Rest when you can, but also power through.

- Everyone allows their boundaries to be crossed now and then. The best you can do is to notice when this has happened and learn from your mistake.
- You're feeling burned out. Recharge, but don't give up.

TEN OF WANDS

VOLATILE VICTORY

GUIDANCE

In succeeding at your goal, you unlocked even more to do. As glorious as this victory may be, it comes with a hefty responsibility and price. You can retain the value of what you have achieved, but you must ask for help, seek balance, and set aside ample downtime to recharge.

It's also a good idea to revisit your values and restructure your efforts accordingly. Now that you have the object of your goal, is it everything you hoped it would be? Or is it less spectacular than it seemed? Maybe there are some aspects of it you want to keep and some you don't care about at all.

Look through the eyes of experience and take stock. Factor in the wisdom you have gained as you decide what it is worth to protect and what values you are ready to release.

Just as it is wise to work hard to achieve a dream, it is also wise to reassess and reapportion where you invest your energy and resources once your initial dream has been achieved.

DYNAMICS

The golden-white phoenix rises out of the searing fire of effort. The creature is dazzling, but it's impossible to ignore how much has been offered up and incinerated for this mystical creature to be born.

What's more, while you (as the phoenix) have nine wands of fire backing you up, you also have one pointed directly at your head.

You can find your way out of this exhausting dynamic, but you must prioritize balance and restructure how you spend your time.

SECRETS

The golden-white phoenix is spiritual gold, formed out of lead and the prolonged effort of the alchemist at work. After all that time in the sweltering workshop, sweaty exhaustion is a natural side product of success.

This energy expenditure is not a cause for regret. Even if your hard-earned success turns out to be not quite as you imagined it, it is better to know it firsthand than to always wonder and pine.

Now, with a greater understanding of the world, you can choose what to let go of, what to keep, and what to focus on next.

MEANINGS AND MESSAGES OF TEN OF WANDS:

- After hard work and furious effort, you finally achieved your dream.
- From your new vantage point of success, prioritize balance as you recharge and reassess.
- Be vigilant in protecting your hard-earned success while also taking time to recharge.
- A non-stop schedule can't be indefinitely maintained.
- Without renewing your energy through rest and contemplation, you are in danger of veering into addiction as your body and mind will look for less healthy forms of respite from the grind.
- Now that you've reached this victory, congratulate yourself, but also take a step back, qualify your values, and find ways to sustainably structure your efforts and time.

MEANINGS AND MESSAGES OF TEN OF WANDS — REVERSED:

- You have burned yourself out or become overwhelmed.
- Rest, recharge, and consider how you can move forward in a more sustainable way.
- Instead of seeing this as a setback, see it as helpful information. Ask yourself — what didn't work before, and what may work better instead?
- No one can work nonstop, and no one enjoys the attempt. Try a different approach.

- A crisis has alerted you to a need for balance. For example, you may be forced to admit an addiction or an abusive relationship dynamic. Choose to see this as an important opportunity to heal.
- In becoming overwhelmed before you reached your goal, you get to ask yourself: do I even want this? If you do, take the scenic route next time. Value not just the destination, but also the experience of getting there.

PRINCESS OF WANDS

YOUTHFUL ADVENTURER

GUIDANCE

Princess of Wands is a young or youthfully enthusiastic adventurer who can't wait to get out into the world and jump into the fray. Watch for a spicy message or a note giving you the go-ahead on something you're passionate about. An impulsive spark will soon ignite into a flame.

Recognize the Princess of Wands' fervor and notice what she is eager to begin. Channel the helpful aspects of this energy but balance it with caution when needed. Identify where this princess shows up in this situation and how she plays a part.

DYNAMICS

The zeal of an initiate is necessary and inspiring, yet it must be tempered. Being on fire for a cause can result in hot-headed and ill-advised action if one does not have the self-awareness to pause and think before boldly moving ahead.

On the other hand, inner fire is what spurs outer progress. Without it, a lack of experience may be used as an excuse to hang back and remain stuck.

You don't need to know everything or see the whole picture before moving forward, but do take a moment to look from multiple angles so you can formulate your tactics and plan. Map out your route, explore your options, and ask for advice from those who have gone before. While you will ultimately choose your own way, it is wise to gather information and weigh the benefits and drawbacks of possible approaches.

Don't strike before you are ready. Temper intensity with prudence. Find the balance between instinctual action and wise inner calm.

S E C R E T S

This young princess is running around with her wand, dreaming of the day she will become a battle-wise warrior. Or, she is the experienced soldier now, and her inner child is sparking her motivation and fueling her passion for her cause.

The symbol for lead above the waxing moon illustrates the transformational energy of the moment. A new creation or condition is in the works. The heaviness of lead is already beginning its transformation into gold.

MEANINGS AND MESSAGES OF PRINCESS OF WANDS:

- A young adventurer or youthful enthusiast has appeared in this situation.
- You are embarking on a new mission or engaging in a new sexual dynamic.
- Expect news about something you're excited about or zealously invested in.
- A new spark of excitement or fire of desire has ignited within you.
- Your inner child or inner adolescent is sparking your joy and enthusiasm.
- You are on fire with a new idea, discipline, project, practice, or area of study.
- You are in the initial stages of a new attraction or sexual dynamic.
- You are being initiated into a group that fights vehemently for something or brings vibrant creations into form.
- You have discovered something new to be enthusiastic about, and now you are raring to go.

MEANINGS AND MESSAGES OF PRINCESS OF WANDS — REVERSED:

- Someone in this situation (maybe you) is behaving like a hothead.
- Take a moment to contemplate and observe before embarking on a new mission or sexual relationship.

- News about something you're excited about or zealously invested in is delayed or not what you hoped it would be.
- Volatile excitement or desire is obscuring your view of the truth.
- Your inner child or inner adolescent is running the show. Embrace all your facets and take your youthful feelings into account, but embody and act from the wise and patient adult.
- Balance your breathless action with downtime, contemplation, and rest.
- Slow down a little so you don't get unwisely carried away by the initial stages of love or attraction.
- Don't blindly follow the values of a group, no matter how invested you are in the cause.
- A person, group, or situation is taking advantage of your zeal. Get honest about this and disengage.

KNIGHT OF WANDS
================

AMBITIOUS HERO

GUIDANCE

This is a fiery person in their 20s or 30s, or a bold and ambitious hero of any age. Passion is stoking the flame of action. Get a running start, grab your wand, and go.

Draw upon your charisma, confidence, and mindful self-mastery. Turn on the charm. Smile, wink, and let your boundless motivation carry you forward on your quest.

Whether the Knight of Wands signifies you or someone else, be aware of his presence in this situation and the fuel he adds to the blaze.

DYNAMICS

The Knight of Wands is the quintessence of being fired up and getting unstuck.

If this card signifies a person, they are on fire with a mission or are in an adventurous phase of life where they are still moving swiftly and learning as they go.

The field is wide open and ready for action. Nothing is holding the Knight of Wands from his journey and quest. His horse is restless and untethered. His wand is ablaze. Rapid action is in the ether, and spectacular transformation is at hand.

The Knight of Wands will do well to ride the current of divine timing. He should act fast without wobbling into sloppy impatience or unnecessary haste.

S E C R E T S

Immediate change is called for, and the knight is poised to be the champion if all goes according to plan.

The sacred geometrical structure of light behind him is electrified. The air is buzzing with potential as the sun rises from beneath the horizon, swift Mercury drifts upward along the diagonal, and expansive Jupiter ascends.

The horse gazes toward the symbol for lead, ready to gallop forward to help bring forth spiritual gold.

All knights carry some of the element of fire, but this knight is double fire. He sparkles with pure dynamism and change. His incandescence cannot be extinguished or contained. It is wild: the more it is exposed to the fresh breeze and open air, the freer and more expansive it becomes.

MEANINGS AND MESSAGES OF KNIGHT OF WANDS:

- A bold person in their 20s or 30s, or an ambitious go-getter of any age, has appeared in this situation.
- This person is on a mission or is in an adventurous and self-defining phase of life.
- Charm and charisma will help you achieve your aim.
- Act swiftly to fire up your success and get unstuck.
- Move forward on your journey or quest.
- Let your passion fuel your expedition.
- Don't hesitate. Act.
- Summon your confidence and take a risk.

MEANINGS AND MESSAGES OF KNIGHT OF WANDS — REVERSED:

- Someone in this situation (maybe you) is feeling overwhelmed by the demands of the moment or the velocity of this present change.
- You may be dealing with someone who is so focused on a mission or adventure, they may not have as much time or energy for you as you'd hoped.
- You are temporarily dazzled by someone's charm and charisma, making it difficult to see who they really are or what they add to the mix.
- You are overthinking this situation, which is causing a delay. Get out of your head, connect with your gut instinct, and make a move.

- You may feel like so much is happening you can't zoom out and see the big picture. Instead of letting this discourage you from acting, put one foot in front of the other and soon you will find your way.
- Temper your passion with patience, but don't let the flame of enthusiasm go out.
- Act fast, but don't act from anxiety or rush things unnecessarily. Strike the right balance between speediness and calm.
- Take a breath, calm your mind, and summon your self-esteem. Then, trust yourself and take a risk.

QUEEN OF WANDS

QUEEN OF WANDS

FABULOUS DIVA

GUIDANCE

The Queen of Wands is a spectacularly fabulous or commanding figure at midlife or beyond, or a charismatic and self-possessed diva of any age. Offer generous support to others through shining your light and sharing your gifts. Be proud of who you are.

Summon your confidence and expand your concept of your potential. Inspire others through your acts of joyful authority. Broadcast your radiance.

Work with and learn from a dynamic and captivating queen-like person, or be that person yourself and bless the world with your unique splendor and sparkle.

DYNAMICS

The Queen of Wands shines like the sun, shedding light and warmth across the surface of the globe. She knows that hiding or minimizing her big personality serves no one, and that her incredible beauty does not take away from anyone else's. In being who she is without pretense or apology, she inspires others to do the same.

The Queen of Wands is astute enough to see that no two people are identical, nor should they be — so proudly embodying one's individuality is the only route to joy.

Our existence is tenuous and unpredictable, so why, the Queen of Wands asks, should we spend a single moment lamenting that we do not look (or act, or talk, or dress) like someone else? Let us instead make the most of this brief sparkle of embers we call life by luxuriating in all that makes us unique.

Our bodies appear in endless variations of shapes and colors and sizes. Our voices each carry a singular resonance and pitch. What we say, and how we want to offer our gifts, are never alike, even with billions of people on earth now and billions who have graced the earth before.

S E C R E T S

There is no end to the queen's power, for she is connected from her crown to the cosmos.

She is demonstrating her personal mastery by balancing on a sphere while appearing calm, collected, and artfully at ease.

Even as she is made of stars, her right eye takes in her immediate earthly surroundings, knowing herself to be entirely infinite even as she looks clearly upon this temporary human realm.

The tree near her is in fact an electrified nerve ending. All her senses are awake, receptive, and on fire.

The symbol for lead hovers on the border of the golden sun because this queen knows how to take solid earthly conditions and transform them into spiritual gold.

MEANINGS AND MESSAGES OF QUEEN OF WANDS:

- A mature or masterful dynamo has appeared in this situation.
- Confidently shine your light and share your gifts.
- Cultivate pride in who you are.
- Draw upon your talents and expand your view of your potential.
- Be yourself unapologetically and inspire others to do so, too.
- Delight in your own beauty and splendor.
- Expand into even more power.
- Take charge of the situation.
- Enjoy wielding your authority.
- Laugh deeply and let your enjoyment of life bless the world.

MEANINGS AND MESSAGES OF QUEEN OF WANDS — REVERSED:

- Someone (maybe you) is acting like a drama queen and causing unnecessary chaos.
- Hiding who you are isn't serving anyone.
- Don't withhold your gifts out of shyness or a false sense of humility.

- Don't waste your life trying to be someone you're not, especially when who you are is so fabulous.
- Don't let anyone intimidate you into being ashamed of or apologizing for who you are or how you show up in the world.
- Love yourself now — stop placing conditions on self-approval.
- Stop minimizing your personal power.
- Admit that you are ready for a leadership role.
- Give yourself permission to be the boss.
- Don't postpone your joy for one moment more.

KING OF WANDS

DRAGON OF TRANSFORMATION

GUIDANCE

A charismatic kingly figure of middle age or older or a socially masterful dynamo of any age has appeared in this situation. Lead boldly, passionately, and with joy. Channel your engaging personality toward creating positive change.

The King of Wands is at ease with influencing others with his winning personality and charm. He trusts his ability to help others feel included and valued. Adept at the social graces and a natural manager of talent and human resources, he knows how to motivate people to join his cause with a welcoming demeanor, a knowing look, or just a wink and a smile.

This king has a heart as warm and bright as the sun, and everyone in his orbit can feel it.

DYNAMICS

Whether it's latent or expressed, hidden or obvious, we all have the potential for confident self-mastery and the ability to gain friends, inspire enthusiasm, and masterfully work a room.

When someone is truly embodying the King of Wands, they aren't just out for attention and accolades (although they may relish in such things). In knowing they hold the power to effect incredible change, their heart is on fire with the desire to help, support, and encourage those around them — their family, their community, or their world.

This, to the King of Wands, is true generosity: shining his light so effusively that all the world is bathed in cheerful illumination and transformational fire.

S E C R E T S

In *The Tarot of Secrets*, the kings are often shapeshifting magicians, and the King of Wands appears here in his spirit animal form as a dragon.

The dragon, like the King of Wands himself, is a creature of luck, dynamism, and transmutation.

He balances effortlessly on a sphere that contains the fire of the alchemist and all the lively elements that actively combine to create spiritual gold. It is a neat package of potentiality: the self-contained globule that contains all he needs to succeed and to bring his desires and wishes into form.

The waning crescent moon tied into the wand illustrates the balance he has achieved. Even though his element is fire and his personality is expansive and bright, he is also attuned to softness, coolness, and receptivity in just the right amounts.

His posture of presence and luxurious ease illustrates his mastery of his element, his craft, and his world.

MEANINGS AND MESSAGES OF KING OF WANDS:

- A charismatic kingly figure has appeared in this situation.
- Enjoy embodying your role as a bold and personable leader.
- Shine your light generously and channel it toward creating positive change.
- Summon your self-confidence.
- You may be called towards activism, particularly in the realms of public speaking or performing.
- Embrace your heart's desire to be seen and appreciated by your community or world for something worthwhile.
- Access your talent to bring out the best in others.
- Use your magic, intention, and charisma to affect dynamic transformation.

MEANINGS AND MESSAGES OF KING OF WANDS — REVERSED:

- Someone in this situation (it could be you) is using charm or persuasiveness in a way that lacks integrity.
- Someone's passionate action is misguided, unbalanced, and volatile.
- Don't hide your light and talents out of a disbelief in the possibility of confidence or a false sense of humility.
- What appears like self-confidence might be narcissism.
- When you're leading, don't just focus on how much attention you can get for your cause — also focus on how to utilize

diverse talents and gifts to practically bring about the change you desire.
- Acknowledge the wounding that spurs your insatiable need for attention.
- Don't hoard the limelight. Share the stage.
- Get clear on what you want to transform or create before you start promoting yourself or gaining followers for your cause.

ACE OF SWORDS

BLADE OF TRUTH

GUIDANCE

Clarity is here. You have uncovered the truth you have been seeking. The sword of illumination has pierced the fog of confusion or indecision, so you now see precisely what is happening and what you need to do.

Speak honestly and take decisive action. If you are already doing so, this card is a sign of validation and a message to continue. Either way, celebrate, for your way forward is now crystal clear.

Sometimes, others will not share your vision or appreciate your honesty. Be kind but firm. Be tough but fair. Be a team player when appropriate, but don't be deterred from taking pivotal action on your own behalf. You are the only one walking your path, so you must trust your inner compass and follow the direction you know to be right.

DYNAMICS

Ace of Swords is the purest and most essential expression of the air element, which is the element of thought, intelligence, swift movement, creative approaches, and new ideas. The inaugural card of the suit, it ushers in a new era of clarity, honesty, and efficiency.

The air element, particularly in this concentrated form, ushers in the winds of change. Let go of heaviness, attachment, and fear. Be bold in carrying out your vision. Let the stuck energy of the past blow away and clear the decks for a bright and beautiful new day.

SECRETS

The snake, here, is a sylph: an air spirit who does not get overly caught up in emotions but rather lives in the realm of whip-smart discernment and levelheaded logic. Draped around your neck, he promotes clear, honest, and articulate language. He helps you express yourself clearly and effectively through speech, creativity, and writing.

On the snake's head, we see the alchemical symbol for daytime. The shadow and mystery of night have parted, the sun is shining, and the clouds, which have been pierced by the sword, are already evaporating into the wide-open sky.

Across from the sun, on the circle, we see the waning moon, which is adjacent to the symbol for air. The watery and heartfelt emotions of the moon are diminishing but are not gone, and they will surely resurge in time. Pure logic is tempered by a dash of compassion and intuition in just the right amount.

MEANINGS AND MESSAGES OF ACE OF SWORDS:

- You can now clearly see and express the truth.
- Your direction is obvious, and your way is open.
- Speak up about your vision or otherwise say what you need to say.
- Express yourself through written or spoken language.
- Now that you know what to do, take swift action.
- Something has shifted, allowing you to align with the energy of authenticity.
- Be bold and move forward in one fell swoop.
- Proceed with logic, discernment, and intelligence.

MEANINGS AND MESSAGES OF ACE OF SWORDS – REVERSED:

- Don't second guess what you know to be true.
- You know what to do, and the way is open, but still you hesitate.
- Stop biting your tongue. While some may not want to hear what you have to say, ultimately, your silence isn't serving anyone.

- Insecurity is keeping you from expressing yourself thoroughly and effectively. Bust through that block without delay.
- Your procrastination isn't serving you. It's time to get moving.
- Truth and clarity are here for you, but you must allow yourself to see them and trust them.
- Be efficient. Don't make things more complicated than they need to be.
- Don't be so carried away by emotion that you can't make a rational choice.

TWO OF SWORDS

THE SPACE BETWEEN

GUIDANCE

There is a wisdom in waiting and a harmony in the space between. As your options are still in the realm of the unmanifest, they are light as air, so there is no purpose in weighing them. Instead, breathe, bide your time, and feel gratitude for your present-moment blessings until your way forward is clear.

During times of transition, there are always moments when we don't know which direction to take or precisely what will unfold. Be present with uncertainty to align with the flow of your luck.

There are many potential outcomes and avenues, and even the tiniest thing can make a huge difference in what eventually unfolds. The alchemist faces this not with fear, but by proactively cultivating a sense that everything is working out perfectly, in divine timing, for the highest and truest good of all.

DYNAMICS

Imagine someone faced with a choice. She considers all the many blessings and drawbacks of each, convincing herself that either choice is great and not so great, in equal amounts but in differing ways. And because she can't predict all possible outcomes, she is unwilling to commit.

Even though this hesitation causes a delay, there is a poised harmony in it. It is not one or the other, and so all possibilities are still present. The pause before the decision has a feather-like lightness because the forthcoming narrative hasn't yet taken any physical form. It is all in the realm of ether: thought, and conjecture; the unknowable and the unknown.

Enjoy this lightness, knowing that you will not stay here forever. Ask the Divine to lead you forward. Trust that when the time is right to act, you will know. And you will know just what to do.

SECRETS

The snow owl is wisdom, soaring confidently through the sparkling dawn.

Beneath one sword's handle is the sun. Beneath the other is the dark moon. This is a masterful balance that demonstrates ease with uncertainty and the spaces between. The future is an adventure.

In between the two handles, we see the alchemical symbol for brass, which is a combination of copper and tin. These are metals of receptivity and expansion. Copper is Venus' metal of luxury and love. Tin is Jupiter's metal of affluence and success.

Sometimes, when we take time with a choice, an option arises that you didn't see or wasn't available before. This may allow you to alchemize the best of both worlds by combining the previous choice's benefits into one.

Above the swords but below the owl, we see the symbol for air and the symbol for iron. These illustrate the power and importance of wisdom, reason, patience, truth, and logical thought.

While the air element is swift moving, this card also urges patience. Things may unfold quickly, but don't rush into a choice unless you are soaring along the air currents of what feels right.

MEANINGS AND MESSAGES OF TWO OF SWORDS:

- Enjoy this moment of mindfulness, possibility, and purposeful contemplation.
- Cultivate clarity and patience so when the way forward presents itself, you will know.
- You are looking at two options, but there may be a third or even a fourth option if you bide your time and look deeply at what you value and desire.
- Be grateful for this feeling of all possibility. Enter the wisdom of uncertainty, and trust that everything is working out for you.
- Look for truth, and then let it guide your way.

MEANINGS AND MESSAGES OF TWO OF SWORDS — REVERSED:

- Don't force things. Take your time. But when you know what you want to do, act.
- Clear clutter and streamline your schedule to establish clarity within.
- Write in a journal or notebook to get clear on what you want and why you want it. This will help you to know which choice to make and to recognize the opportunity that is best for you.
- There is freedom and adventure in uncertainty, if only you will be brave enough to see it.
- Be honest and admit the truth you already know.

THREE OF SWORDS

PURIFYING PAIN

GUIDANCE

Heartbreak is a purifying agent which, in time, provides you with healing, wisdom, and a greater capacity to love. All deep love includes and requires moments of acute pain. So, embrace your pain — welcome it, bless it, and allow it to transform you to your very core.

You can't escape sorrow at this time, so you may as well dive straight into the center of it. Breathe into your feelings. Surrender to what's happening. Let the pain remind you that you're living bravely, you're living fully, and you're completely and courageously alive.

In this way, you will perform the alchemy that will transform you, elevate you, and eventually deliver you to your next adventure and beautiful life stage.

DYNAMICS

Three of Swords is too often feared and unfairly maligned, for love is what makes life worth living, and pain is what alerts us to the presence of love. Consider a beloved child, parent, or animal friend. Even when this being is thriving, when you feel your love for them, you also feel an ache, for you know they will not live forever, and they will certainly suffer moments of loneliness, struggle, sorrow, and physical pain.

Alchemists know that even the darkest night makes way for the glorious dawn, and in fact that the dawn's very existence depends upon the night. Alchemical wisdom also teaches us that a violent storm leads to a healthy forest, a raging fire burns away the dead wood, and lead contains all the ingredients necessary for gold.

Live your life with this wisdom, and you need fear nothing. Whatever happens will be grist for the mill — a reminder that you are living with a wide-open heart and soaking in all the beauty and magic of this mysterious human experience.

SECRETS

A heart pierced with swords is not just a symbol of pain, but also a symbol of passion and care. It is not so different, after all, from a heart pierced with Cupid's arrow: a universal symbol for being in love.

Everyone you love is their own creature, with their own preferences and personality. At times, they will each desire things that are not in alignment with your desires. They will hurt you by something they do or don't do, something they say or don't say, or something they want or don't want.

Hide from or attempt to escape this heartache at your peril. For while it may close you off from your anguish, it will most certainly close you off from your joy.

Be willing to undergo the agony and you will experience the ecstasy. This is a secret of unspeakable value. Live and die by it, and you will be flush with spiritual gold.

MEANINGS AND MESSAGES OF THREE OF SWORDS:

- Breathe into heartbreak and sorrow and let it purify your soul.
- Be brave enough to feel your feelings.
- Accept that love requires pain. Be willing to suffer through this painful period for the sake of love.
- A relationship is causing your heart to ache, for there is great love in your heart.
- Fear nothing, feel everything, and remember that love is the cause of it all. Do this and you will sense and become one with the underlying perfection of all that is.
- Feeling your pain will inspire you, heal you, and align you with great power.

MEANINGS AND MESSAGES OF THREE OF SWORDS — REVERSED:

- You are in denial about heartbreak, sorrow, or disappointment. Admit it, feel it, and let it purify you.
- In only being willing to feel pleasant feelings, you are numbing out and living your life halfway.
- Stop judging your loved ones and accept them as they are instead, even if their actions are hurting you or have hurt you in the past. You can certainly set boundaries, and be honest about your feelings, but start by accepting things the way they are.
- Stop believing things "shouldn't have happened" or "should have happened" a certain way. Instead, come into alignment with what is already true, and go from there.
- Don't place conditions on reality. Fighting against what is already true is a battle you have already lost.
- You can feel your feelings without being stuck in them forever. In fact, it is only in feeling them that they will begin to dissolve.

FOUR OF SWORDS

REST AND RECHARGE

GUIDANCE

You have done enough for now. Quiet your mind and spend time alone to recalibrate and recharge. Rest, pure and simple, will heal you, restore your enthusiasm, and provide you with the perspective you need.

You have been undergoing significant stress. This stress may be related to a big and happy change, or it may be in response to discord, drama, or a grievous loss. It also may be that you're encountering a mix of desirable conditions and undesirable ones, making for a chaotic time filled with a mix of excitement and pleasure, exhaustion and strife.

Whatever the source and form of your stress, take a break. You've done all that you can do for now, so the best thing you can do in this moment is rest.

Go somewhere quiet. Lovingly tend to rest-related self-care concerns, such as washing your sheets, showering or bathing, and establishing a nurturing environment in which to recharge. Hydrate and nourish your body with plenty of fluids and healthy food. Minimize distractions, put on some clean and cozy clothing, and find a comfortable spot to recline.

Read a novel or do a crossword puzzle if you like. Just don't do anything too useful, frenetic, or intellectually strenuous. Detach from digital distractions. Your mind, much like your body, needs a holiday.

DYNAMICS

Without stress of any kind, you would be bored and get stuck in a rut. But too much stress for too long without a break leads to burnout. Just like every living thing, you can't thrive without the nourishment you need. Rest is nourishment. So is loving and attentive self-care.

Now is a time to look at what is inside and outside of your locus of control. Once you've done all you can do, you must let go and take some time to relax so you can replenish your energy, clarity, and personal power.

SECRETS

This maiden's red shoes are symbols of her mystical nature and her intrinsic energetic connection to the Great Goddess and Mother Earth. She wears a nightgown inscribed with sacred symbols of power and regeneration. The moon beneath her recharges her spiritual batteries, filling her with the cool light of magic and intuitive wisdom.

The four swords point downward towards her and grow roots. She is in the underworld and soil, but also in the ancient and primordial cosmos: the transcendent, subterranean, and regenerative land of dreams.

MEANINGS AND MESSAGES OF FOUR OF SWORDS:

- The best thing you can do right now is rest.
- In letting go of what you can't control, you enlist the help of the universe.
- When you quiet your mind and let your body be still, miracles and magic will flow in.
- You are completely justified in taking some time off for relaxation and peaceful and unhurried forms of play.
- Your intuition will come back online when you reduce distractions, care for yourself lovingly, and take some time away from your computer, phone, and the daily grind.

MEANINGS AND MESSAGES OF FOUR OF SWORDS – REVERSED:

- You have been ignoring your physical and spiritual needs for quiet time and rest.
- Stop trying to force things. If you could see the big picture, you would know that everything is in divine and perfect order.
- You've been going so hard for so long, it's as if you have forgotten how to rest. But the minute you remind yourself,

things will begin to flow in the right direction all on their own.
- You are minimizing your challenges and hard work. Acknowledge them so you can treat yourself to the loving self-care you need.
- You're so harried or sleep-deprived, you've lost touch with your spiritual guidance system. But you can reconnect with it easily just as soon as you get some rest.

FIVE OF SWORDS

THERE MUST BE A WAY

GUIDANCE

Think creatively and take an unconventional approach. When you act resourcefully and trust in the magic of the universe, you will open a portal of possibility. You needn't follow all the rules to the letter, provided you are impeccable in your alignment with your own inner compass.

Whether you assume you have no options, or whether you assume you have an abundance of options, you will find yourself to be correct. So, begin now to expect a wonderful turn of events that is beyond your present ability to foresee.

Be hopeful, sporting, and joyfully expectant. Be bold. Be fearless. Look past surface appearances to see the hidden opportunities that lie beneath. Be wily and wise.

You may need to bluff a little to get from where you are to where you want to be. Wherever you are or want to be, behave as if you know you belong there. Say yes with conviction, even if you don't quite know what that affirmative will eventually entail. Speak confidently and take bold action, even if you've never encountered such a challenge in the past. Dress and act as if you already have the degree of success you would like to possess.

After all, you *do* belong. You *are* qualified. You are entitled to manifest your desires. As many times as necessary, remind yourself — *if other people have achieved this degree of success, why shouldn't I?*

D Y N A M I C S

It's likely you can look back and see that time and again, the universe has presented you with miraculous blessings and unexpected windfalls. Just when you started to think you had no options, an option appeared — seemingly out of nowhere at all. When you grabbed it and ran with it, it turned out to be the best of all possible circumstances for your personal evolution and earthly needs.

This, too, can be one of those times.

The five swords point down into the earth, creating a ring of fire and a portal to the stars where before there was only the appearance of soil and sod.

But heed this caveat: do not misuse your resourcefulness. Do not selfishly take advantage of others. Getting creative with the rules is fine, provided you do no harm. While it's true that ethics are in many ways subjective, you know in your heart what does and does not feel right.

SECRETS

Five teardrops fall from the swords through the subterranean cosmos. Moving forward brings heartache, even when the movement is positive and necessary. The crescent moon, upside down, is a symbol of protection. In bringing forth positive change, you shield yourself from the negative effects of staying stuck and enlist the protective power of the universe.

In the upper left corner is the symbol for day: as the portal of possibility opens, the sun rises on positive and auspicious new conditions. In the upper right corner is the symbol for the air element, which is aligned with the suit of swords, as well as intellect, words, rules, and the power of the thinking mind.

MEANINGS AND MESSAGES OF FIVE OF SWORDS:

- Think creatively and believe in your ability to manifest positive change.
- Look for opportunities and act on them.
- Bluff a little to get from where you are to where you want to be.
- Bend the rules without harming or taking advantage of others.

MEANINGS AND MESSAGES OF FIVE OF SWORDS — REVERSED:

- Possibilities are here for you, but you haven't allowed yourself to see them yet.
- Don't assume that you can't succeed. Assume you can. Then be attentive to intuitive nudges and signs.
- Don't wait to feel bold before you behave boldly. Let your actions inform your feelings rather than the other way around.
- Be honest with yourself about the difference between harmless rule bending and harmful deceit.

SIX OF SWORDS
SAFE PASSAGE

GUIDANCE

After a challenging time, you are on your way to safety. After struggle, you are on your way to peace. It may feel like you are moving at a snail's pace, but that is an illusion — things are progressing more swiftly and ideally than they seem.

You have worked hard to get away from a particular challenge or living situation, and to propel yourself toward a safer and more harmonious realm. And you have indeed set things in motion according to your will. Now, you must relax and let yourself be carried forward by life, by your spiritual support system, and by helpful allies, family members, and friends.

Congratulate yourself for doing all you can do. You identified the problem or the situation that needed to be changed. Then, you made the necessary arrangements and enlisted the appropriate support. Now, rest, and let the momentum you have built propel you in the direction you have chosen.

DYNAMICS

There is an invisible field of light and information that informs and defines all things: recording and projecting your soul's journey through time and holding the structure of reality as we know it in place.

When you choose, you can alter your life trajectory by reaching in and affecting positive change in this energetic field. You can do so with your intention and actions, and by consciously choosing new and more empowering habits, energetic qualities, beliefs, expectations, and paradigms.

This is a working definition of spiritual alchemy and conscious personal evolution.

Congratulations, for you have successfully attuned your aura and energetic record to the frequency of your desire and chosen trajectory.

Now, rest in the boat as it sails along the route you have mapped out.

Of course, you must still be sensitive to your inner guidance and act on it. But mostly, you must let yourself be carried forward, out of the treacherous waters and into the calm and sparkling sea.

SECRETS

The symbol for daylight mirrors the dissipation of struggle and the dawn of a new day.

In response to a clear and focused intention, the swords—symbols of thought and the air element—all point in the same direction, efficiently carrying the boat forward into peace.

The symbol for the air element hovers in the upper right corner.

MEANINGS AND MESSAGES OF SIX OF SWORDS:

- As a result of your past focus, intention, and hard work, you are moving more quickly than you realize, in precisely the direction you desire.
- The bulk of the challenge is behind you. Calmer and more pleasant conditions are ahead.
- You have already set this change in motion. Now, relax and let yourself be carried forward.
- Be alert to your intuitive guidance and to what feels right, but mostly let others support you. Spirit is leading your boat to safety.
- Rest and recharge even as you continue to move forward toward greater peace.
- You may be traveling somewhere or moving to a new home.

MEANINGS AND MESSAGES OF SIX OF SWORDS — REVERSED:

- Recalibrate your compass and revise your direction. You know where you want to go, but you haven't been heading that way.

- You can put this challenge behind you, but first you must make an adjustment in your perspective and behavior.
- You don't have to keep revisiting the same problem again and again. First, change your beliefs and expectations. Then, enlist the help you need.
- A mental block is keeping you stuck. Recognize it and release it, and you can turn this boat around.
- You can rest and recharge, but only once you navigate in a new direction. Until you do so, you will continue to experience unpleasant shakeups.
- You may be traveling or moving in response to an unexpected upheaval. This is a wakeup call and blessing in disguise.

SEVEN OF SWORDS

DETECT THE CON

GUIDANCE

Someone may be deceiving you, or you may be deceiving someone else. Stay in, or come back to, integrity: don't cross the line between wily and fraudulent; crafty and devious. All is not what it seems, but you will find your way by the guiding light of your intuition and your honor.

Bring your schemes and agendas out of hiding and be honest with yourself about what you want and what is driving your behavior. Look closely to see where others may be acting in a duplicitous or untrustworthy way.

This card may be an indication that you have taken something that was not yours to take, or you have plans to do so soon. Or it could be alerting you to the fact that someone has taken something valuable from you or may be intending to do so.

D Y N A M I C S

Like the fox, the human is a wily animal. There are times when we feel the need to be sneaky, or spin a tall tale, or add flourishes that stretch and obscure the truth.

As a social species, we have learned there is often value in portraying a certain image of who we are, what we are up to, and why we are doing what we do. What's more, we learn and share wisdom with stories and narratives.

But while storytelling and mythmaking are natural and vital aspects of our shared culture, there are times when they veer into manipulation and exploitation, and in turn create more problems than they solve.

You can have compassion for yourself, and everyone concerned, even as you readjust your perception to see what is really going on. We all make mistakes, we all fall victim to deception, and we all, at times, get carried away.

If you are bitter, embarrassed, or ashamed, remember that these feelings and the conditions that cause them are universal to the human experience. You are not alone. Part of exposing the truth includes exposing how you feel. Breathe into these feelings and let them heal.

Learn from this situation and, ultimately, it will bolster your wisdom and your strength.

SECRETS

Even as this fox has been turned upside down and has his head in a cloud of fog, the alchemical symbol for day hovers nearby, illustrating that he has the potential to arise into the light and see what is really going on.

At the same time, his head is pointed directly at the moon, and the point of a sword. In this case, the moon symbolizes instability, and the sword, imminent danger. To emerge unscathed, he must proactively shift his trajectory — and soon.

MEANINGS AND MESSAGES OF SEVEN OF SWORDS:

- Be mindful of potential theft or deception.
- Being creative is fine, but don't be dishonest or exploitative. You know where the line is.
- Correct your course to align with integrity.
- You may be dealing with a con-person, or you could be behaving like one yourself.
- Something is not on the up-and-up.
- Realign with your intuition and you will know what you need to do.

MEANINGS AND MESSAGES OF SEVEN OF SWORDS — REVERSED:

- You have detected theft or deception.
- Your dishonesty or self-serving behavior has finally caught up with you.
- Now that you've been caught, the best you can do is confess, make amends, and earnestly realign with your integrity.
- The dishonest behavior of someone you trusted has been exposed.
- You have finally seen through someone's deception, or your own misrepresentations have been revealed.
- That which was out of integrity has collapsed.
- Now that you know what's really going on, realign your inner compass, and restructure your plan.

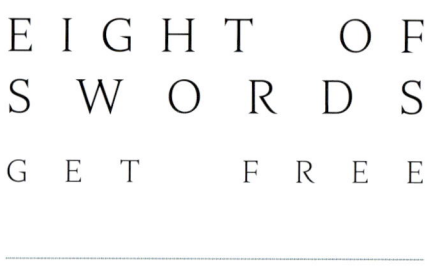

EIGHT OF SWORDS

GET FREE

GUIDANCE

Mental barriers must be released. Freedom is here for you, but you must see your way out of a trap. Your prison is not physical but is made entirely of thought.

Will you get out or remain stuck? It is an inner journey, not an outer one. The outcome can go either way, and getting from where you are now to where you want to be is entirely up to you.

Don't give up, and don't take this situation at face value. There is a way out.

Imagine lying on your deathbed, looking back on your life from your final moments. This will help you see the thought patterns that were never necessary or helpful, so you can free yourself from your present mental trap.

It's a good idea to take a long bath or a contemplative walk outside by yourself. Breathe consciously as you take some time out to meditate, quantify, and observe.

D Y N A M I C S

You thought you were leaping forward, and maybe you were. But then you found yourself hovering in midair, unable to move forward, backward, left, or right. This pause is allowing you to see the unhelpful narrative or unhealthy obsession that has been governing your perception.

Perhaps you have been wasting precious thought energy on something that doesn't really matter, such as your weight, or your status, or another false marker of your worth.

Even if the problem seems to be tangible and external, it mirrors an inner challenge, and can therefore be solved with an inner solution.

You may be tempted to see yourself as a victim of your present circumstance. Instead, choose to see it as a perfect opportunity to evolve.

In one way or another, you have been looking at things one way, when there is a more useful and productive way to perceive.

S E C R E T S

The eight swords are strategically positioned in such a way to create a holding space: a circle or bubble of thought and energy, surrounded by ley lines and presently unrealized alchemical potential.

On the one hand, this is a spirit trap. On the other, it is a sacred container. Both are true, but if you want to unlock the potential and get yourself out, you must throw off your inner encumbrances and transcend the tired old stories that have been holding you back.

This horse has always been made of stardust, with a mind on fire with divine clarity and light. She may have forgotten that for a moment, but this situation is providing her with everything she needs to remember it again.

MEANINGS AND MESSAGES OF EIGHT OF SWORDS:

- See things in a new way, and you will free yourself from limitations and traps.
- You feel temporarily trapped, but the outcome is up to you: call on Spirit for help and think your way free.
- Rise up and out of the mental pattern that is draining you and keeping you stuck.
- This situation may seem like a puzzle or a trap, but it is providing you with the impetus to bust out of an old rut and be free.
- An external problem mirrors an internal confusion. Start in the realm of thought and perception, for this is where the solution can be found.

MEANINGS AND MESSAGES OF EIGHT OF SWORDS – REVERSED:

- You are already seeing things in a new way, and it is freeing you.

- Congratulations: you called on Spirit and found your way out of an inner trap.
- You have finally succeeded at releasing a mental pattern that has been draining you.
- You solved a puzzle and broke out of a trap.
- You are transforming a problem by choosing a new focus and lens of perception.

NINE OF SWORDS

CONQUER YOUR FEAR

GUIDANCE

Leap boldly across the chasm of worry and despair. Clarity has revealed the problem so you can finally face it. You need live in fear no longer, as you are now ready to address the issue, which will in turn allow you to move your story along.

As uncomfortable as it may be to admit the challenge you face, it's also a victory, because it gives you the opportunity to heal and evolve.

The secret is this: dare to trust yourself. You are ready. You are qualified. Adopt a proactive and patient problem-solving mindset, and you will sort out the puzzle and conquer your fear.

DYNAMICS

As much as we all crave ease, a life confined to the cliff of comfort is the quintessence of boredom, never pushing us to explore or expand.

Luckily, to steer you clear of such stagnation, the nine shining swords of destiny are here to threaten you with their treacherous blades, forcing you to step out of old thought patterns and make a move.

This is a portal to a new reality for you. After inner struggle, you will find outer calm. But only if you release unhelpful stories and outmoded ways of thinking so you can sort out the practical challenges of the issue and dwell in the simple perfection of the now.

S E C R E T S

On one side of the cliff, you cling to ideas of what should be or what should have been: how your life should have gone, what things should look like, and how others should behave. On the other, you accept what is true and calmly take stock of what is already in place.

This is the realm of the present moment, exactly as it is.

That is where you can thrive. That is where you will be free.

In this realm, should you choose to leap into it, whatever arises, you deal with it. If you need help, you ask for it. If you need to learn something new, you study it. Inevitably, you trust that you are divinely guided, holistically supported, and more than equal to the situation at hand.

MEANINGS AND MESSAGES OF NINE OF SWORDS:

- Breathe, calm your mind, and call on divine support. Then, act.
- You can heal this situation if you stop ruminating and face your problems head on.
- Release attachment to stories about how things should be and accept them as they are. This will clear your mind and give you the wisdom you need to proceed.
- Clinging to resentment has been holding you back, but it need do no longer.
- We all feel hurt and confused sometimes. But now it's time to patch things up and move on.
- Stay focused on the things you can control and stop wasting thought energy on the things you can't.
- Clear your mind of overthinking and boldly deal with the situation at hand.

MEANINGS AND MESSAGES OF NINE OF SWORDS – REVERSED:

- You have cleared your mind of worry and successfully aligned with the Divine.
- Bold action has cleared your path and freed you from excessive worry and fear.
- Accepting things as they are and letting go of old stories is propelling you into a beautiful new phase.
- Letting go of resentment is freeing your soul.

- You faced a challenge and found your way out of a trap.
- By concentrating on the things within your locus of control, you empowered yourself, shifted your momentum, and found your way.
- Proactively dealing with a problem or challenge has cleared the path to inner freedom, which will unlock a new level of success.

TEN OF SWORDS

INEVITABLE END

GUIDANCE

That's it — it's over. The situation has run its course. After all that struggling, over-analyzing, and keeping yourself up at night, an era is finally ending, and a cycle has become complete.

Whether or not you want to admit it, there is nothing else to try and nowhere else to go. The best you can do is close the door behind you and courageously move on.

While pain and regret are likely present, closing this chapter is ideal and will ultimately turn out for the best. It will provide an opportunity to heal, learn from your mistakes, and eventually begin again.

This may be the end of a relationship, career, project, hope, dream, plan, or living situation. Perhaps you ended it or need to end it, or perhaps someone or something ended it for you. Either way, remember that every ending is also a beginning, and with each cycle we complete, we learn.

Even if this conclusion isn't the happy or victorious one you had hoped for and envisioned, trust that it is the right one for this cycle. Things happen as they happen, and it follows that they should not have happened any other way.

The sooner you can embrace this, the sooner the new cycle can begin.

DYNAMICS

The journey of swords has come full circle: from breath of conception, to all the ups and downs of outsmarting and overthinking, to this inevitable heart-piercing denouement.

But an ending is not synonymous with failure. If you resist the urge to judge the entire journey by the ending, you will see that you have evolved, matured, and learned vital lessons along the way.

SECRETS

A heart stabbed with swords will never feel good. But from the compost of conflict and confusion, a beautiful flower will grow.

You may feel naked, vulnerable, and alone, on your own little planet of despair. But look through eyes of courage, and you will find a lily of hope to plant in the fertile soil beneath your toes.

And when a new cycle begins (which it will), you will have more wisdom to work with. Your experience will give you nuance, and the depth of your past sorrow will have carved out a deeper aptitude for your joy.

MEANINGS AND MESSAGES OF TEN OF SWORDS:

- It's over. Say goodbye and move on.
- Cut ties and stop trying to resuscitate a cycle that has reached its inevitable end.
- Don't fight your sadness or disappointment. Feel it so you can make peace with this ending and prepare for something beautiful and new.
- There was something you didn't expect or plan for, or you are just now realizing you were deceived by others or deceived yourself. Don't inwardly punish yourself and don't dwell.
- Remember: it's not just you. Everyone runs into disappointment, deception, heartbreak, and loss. Have compassion with yourself, reassess, and consider your next move.
- This change or ending may feel painful, but it will ultimately be for the best.

MEANINGS AND MESSAGES OF TEN OF SWORDS — REVERSED:

- Move with this change rather than against it.
- A crisis of logistics or the heart has swept in and upended everything you thought you knew.
- Sometimes fate has other plans for you. Roll with the changes as best you can and hidden blessings will be revealed.

- The sooner you can surrender to this change, the sooner you will regain your bearings and discover new avenues and opportunities for growth.
- Be engaged and interested in what this turn of events has in store.
- If someone has broken your heart, stop trying to convince them to change their mind. Let things be so you can begin to heal.

PRINCESS OF SWORDS

ADOLESCENT VISIONARY

GUIDANCE

The Princess of Swords is a young writer or thinker, or someone of any age who is engaging with words and ideas in a youthful way. A clear written or spoken message may appear soon. A new perspective born from intellectual thought and philosophical understanding will breeze through, elevate your mind, and affect positive change.

Zoom out and see the big picture. Study, research, and plan. Identify where the Princess of Swords is showing up in this situation and take note of how she plays a part.

DYNAMICS

The mind is a powerful and precarious thing. Human thought can solve seemingly insurmountable problems, but it can also turn on itself, leading to anxiety, confusion, and unrest.

The Princess of Swords is all up in her head. She will do well to remember that she doesn't need to understand everything —

in fact, she couldn't even if she tried. But she can take care of her mental space and protect her sanity by grounding herself in her body and attending to the practical and tangible details of her physical world.

Look clearly at the messages you are receiving from outside yourself and reinforcing in your own mind. Make sure the stories others are telling you and the stories you are telling yourself are helpful, supportive, and true. Question assumptions but stay solid. Draw upon the creative power of your imagination but try not to get dazzled by a beautiful illusion or dissolve into a dream.

S   E   C   R   E   T   S

The sword opens a portal to infinity, allowing for sparkling insight to shine through. Yet, in hovering so high above the ground, the princess strains her connection to everyday practicality and truth.

She may bring valuable messages and helpful concepts, or she may get too caught up in the realm of ideas and carried away.

A thoughtful adolescent or an adult who is in a cycle of youthfully rethinking her world, the Princess of Swords can be a force of positive change, but she must guard against getting lost in surreal illusions or the perils of her own dogmatic overthinking. She must do her best to sort out what is real from what is oversimplification or a dream.

MEANINGS AND MESSAGES OF PRINCESS OF SWORDS:

- A young or youthful writer or thinker has appeared in this situation.
- A new perspective or understanding is making an appearance in your mind.
- Thoroughly research your options and contemplate your next move before you act.
- Expect a significant spoken or written communication.
- Your thoughts are buzzing and new ideas are inspiring you to take action.
- You are taken with a new ideology, philosophy, or mental discipline.
- You have an idea for a verbal project such as an article, book, or spoken presentation.
- You are joining a group of philosophers, thinkers, or idealistic activists.
- You are embarking on a new mental discipline or area of study.

MEANINGS AND MESSAGES OF PRINCESS OF SWORDS — REVERSED:

- A young person or a person of any age who is experiencing an idealistic or philosophical renaissance (maybe you) is getting carried away.
- Question a new perspective or approach before assuming it is correct.

- Don't act rashly. First, think things through.
- A spoken or written communication is delayed or not what you expected.
- Breathe, slow down, and ground your energy in the physical world before frenetic thought untethers you from practical wisdom.
- Take a new ideology or philosophy with a grain of salt.
- Take some time to plan your project before you begin.
- Even if a group seems to share your perspective, continue to think critically and to be the sole gatekeeper of your own mind.
- Proactively curb overthinking and worry.

KNIGHT OF SWORDS

KNIGHT OF SWORDS
VALIANT VISIONARY

G U I D A N C E

This is a bold and intelligent person in their 20s or 30s, or an impulsive visionary of any age. The Knight of Swords is ready to jump in and go. This is a time to outsmart your opponent, get a jump on the competition, and use your shining sword to cut through deliberations and delays.

Breathe deeply and cultivate a relaxed alertness to keep your mind clear and your reactions agile. This will support you in knowing just what to do and then doing it — precisely when the time is right.

On the other hand, the time may already be right. If this is the case, don't hesitate — get moving. The wisdom you need is here for you. Access it, realize it, and act on it posthaste.

D Y N A M I C S

The Knight of Swords has no time for fear. She has already done her due diligence through hard work, physical preparation, and learning to calm her mind. To embody her full potential, she knows she must inhabit her body and call upon the Divine for support. Then, she must listen to her intuition, trust her training, and let sacred momentum propel her to her goal.

She is like an athlete who has diligently practiced and is now at the most crucial moment of a game. Even as she is in motion, she must clear her mind of thought and let pure focus and mind-body wisdom carry her through.

Whether the Knight of Swords signifies you or someone else, be aware of her presence in this situation and the bracing air current of change she breathes into the wind.

S E C R E T S

The Knight of Swords has just sliced through a cloud of confusion, demolishing its power and establishing clarity in its wake.

Now, her sword's point rests in the center of the white-hot sun as it cleanses and recharges in the atomic fire.

Behind the knight, the alchemical symbol for day illustrates that as clarity dawns, it demolishes the darkness of confusion utterly.

She is clothed in the cosmos for her action is unbounded and her determination is vast.

Her horse's countenance is calm, even as his posture is electrified. He is alert, present, and raring to go.

MEANINGS AND MESSAGES OF KNIGHT OF SWORDS:

- A heroic and intelligent person in their 20s or 30s, or an impulsive visionary of any age has appeared in this situation.
- Act swiftly and decisively.
- Combine conviction with rapid action to defend what (or whom) you care about.
- Align your mind, body, and spirit, and act immediately.
- Be proactive about getting unstuck and busting through delays.
- Combine your intelligence with action.

MEANINGS AND MESSAGES OF KNIGHT OF SWORDS — REVERSED:

- Someone in this situation (maybe you) has what they need to succeed, but first they must stop briefly to contemplate their next move.
- Take a deep breath, get clear on your intention, and invoke divine support. Then (and only then) decisively proceed.
- Before you advance, stop and examine your motives. What do you want, and why? Adjust your answers as needed and let them inform your next move.
- Take a step back to align your mind, body, and spirit. Focus your mind, practice your craft, and stay sharp. When it's obviously time to jump back into the action, do it.
- Sometimes acting speedily is called for. Other times, haste causes more delays than it avoids. Take a beat to find your

footing and get clear on your intentions. This will get you into divine harmony and flow.
- Action without intelligence is unwise. Performance without practice is unreliable. Take heed and plan ahead.

QUEEN OF SWORDS

CHANNEL OF INTEGRITY

GUIDANCE

This is a wise, intelligent, and authoritative person at middle age or older or a queenlike professional of any age. Connect with your compassion but also set boundaries, be disciplined, and clarify the rules. Rise above drama, cut through confusion, and be a conduit of divine integrity and balance.

Look for the messages hidden in this situation and be honest about all that you already know. Feel your feelings but don't let them overtake you. Be willing to make some hard decisions. Establish lightness and beauty in your inner and outer worlds.

Some of this queen's wisdom is learned, but much of it is channeled straight from the sky, the heavens, and the realm of the gods.

DYNAMICS

The Queen of Swords is not worried about appearing authoritative, for she is too busy being authoritative. This is her way, for she is naturally and intrinsically aligned with the purest truth and highest justice of the land.

Letting her feelings flow through her, her job is often a hard one for she takes both her heart and her mind into account with every action and choice. She knows that when she consults her heart but lets her mind have the final say, justice will be served in the best possible way for all concerned.

The heart, when left to its own devices, may counsel you to overextend yourself, commit to a beautiful but deceptive partner, or deny your very real needs. The mind will recognize such traps and help you sidestep or find your way out of them.

This queen knows that heartache, in this lifetime, is inevitable, and we must not seek to avoid it at all costs, for this will compromise our very well-being.

SECRETS

The Green Lion is an alchemical mythological being who eats the sun, unceremoniously assimilating the secret wisdom hidden in the external world. The Red Lion symbolizes fully realized power and passion. Together, their respective colors form this queen's vehicle for wisdom — they provide the perpetual motion and dynamic balance that allow her to soar above the confusion and the fray.

Her posture is relaxed and open to spirit. Although her heart may ache, she is accustomed to keeping it open to the sky. Her mind, too, is relaxed and open, prepared to override her heart's yearnings when necessary for the sake of justice, her own well-being, and the truest good of all concerned.

MEANINGS AND MESSAGES OF QUEEN OF SWORDS:

- An intelligent queen-like person or authoritative professional has appeared in this situation.
- Rule with clarity, impartiality, and calm.
- Prioritize fairness, justice, and balance.
- Set boundaries and clarify rules.
- Be decisive.
- Keep your heart open while maintaining discipline and structure.
- Tap into divine wisdom and take all your knowledge into account.
- As you contemplate your next move, study and learn everything you can.
- Consider all the angles.
- Establish lightness and beauty in your world.
- Take the lead and lay the groundwork for your success.

MEANINGS AND MESSAGES OF QUEEN OF SWORDS — REVERSED:

- Someone (maybe you) is being deceptive, tricky, or vindictive.
- You or someone else in this situation is acting out of jealousy or envy.
- You can't please or appease everyone. Be compassionate but firm.
- Don't let fulfilling the needs of others allow you to ignore or devalue your own.
- Consult your own inner knowing and get clear on what you believe, desire, and need.
- Poor planning or excessive permissiveness is derailing your success — get better habits, boundaries, and priorities in place.
- Don't get carried away by an illusion — look more deeply, discover the truth, and make choices accordingly.
- Intuition and instinct are great, but right now you also need to know facts.
- Before you rush ahead, look for other possible options and approaches.
- Clear clutter and establish beauty through elegant minimalism.
- Don't let others make your choices for you.

KING OF SWORDS

MASTER OF TRUTH

GUIDANCE

The King of Swords is a decisive, intelligent, authoritative figure at midlife or older, or an efficient and confident thought leader of any age. Ideas, choices, and power dynamics are of the essence now. Attune your reasoning faculties with divinity and ally your actions with integrity, clear perception, and truth.

Although the King of Swords feels things deeply, he does not allow his emotions to sway his decrees. He knows that as an arbiter of justice, he must be impartial. He does not ignore or deny his feelings, but he acts with impeccable calm and lets cool logic run the show.

At the same time, there is an intuitive aspect to the King of Swords. Connecting with the infinite, he gains access to more information and higher levels of thought processing, which aligns his logic, ethics, and problem-solving capabilities with the realm of the divine.

DYNAMICS

It takes practice to consistently distinguish between beliefs and facts, hunches and conclusions. But when one is a master like the King of Swords, an added degree of power is present. Even in the middle of a challenge, you can perceive clearly and choose what to do from a place of inner peace. You can stop wasting energy on all that you can't control so you can efficiently channel your attention toward all that you can.

The King of Swords wastes no time people pleasing or sticking around when he wants or needs to be elsewhere. He sees no reason to behave misleadingly to make others feel at ease. He has no problem saying "goodbye," "I don't like that," and "no way." It is not that he is rude, but rather that he sees dishonesty in the name of politeness as a form of manipulation. He would not want others to sugarcoat things to please him, so he treats others as he wants to be treated: with efficiency and the plainest spoken truth.

SECRETS

This is the King of Swords in his eagle form. His head does not appear because it is one with the sky — it contains all air currents of reason and all particulates of truth.

Rubedo—the red elixir of life—drips from the full moon to the laurel vine of victory, where it becomes the simplest of fluids and the basis of all life on earth, which is water. The water symbolizes the purity of logic and impartiality.

Beneath the sword point, *rubedo* drops into the abyss of the cosmos. Beneath the sword's hilt shines the sun. The alchemical sign for the sunrise hovers in the lower left corner. With the clarity of the early morning sun, the King of Swords offers nourishment to all beings.

MEANINGS AND MESSAGES OF KING OF SWORDS:

- A decisive and intelligent authoritative figure at middle age or older or an efficient thought leader of any age has appeared in this situation.
- Align your thoughts and decisions with the essence of divine truth.
- Be calm, logical, and impartial, but also let your intuition guide your thinking.
- Be efficient in your thoughts and actions by focusing on what you can control and letting go of what you can't.
- Manage your time and energy economically.
- Lead fairly and speak plainly.
- Employ your calm intelligence when deciding your next move.

MEANINGS AND MESSAGES OF KING OF SWORDS – REVERSED:

- Someone in this situation (it could be you) is using their intelligence in a dishonorable and manipulative way.

- Don't just act on behalf of yourself — prioritize the highest good for all concerned.
- Even if you let rationality guide you, don't completely ignore your feelings.
- Don't waste time or mental energy worrying about things you can't control.
- Unequivocally set boundaries around your time and energy.
- Determine what is fair and just before you proceed.
- Be decisive but think before you act and let logic have the final say.

ACE OF COINS
LUCKY BUNNY

GUIDANCE

Wealth and abundance are manifesting. An opportunity for affluence is here or on the horizon. This is a stage of incredible growth, possibility, and luck.

A harbinger of incredible fortune, Ace of Coins is the purest and most essential expression of the earth element.

This card bodes well for whatever you're asking about. Your money is multiplying. Opportunities abound. A business venture will gloriously succeed. The universe is on your side, the earth supports you, and everything is going your way.

DYNAMICS

Just as magical herbs and dew are harvested at the Midsummer sunrise to encapsulate and channel the magic of the brightest and most expansive day of the year, Ace of Coins is a manifestation of the richest and most nourishing bounty of the earth, ether, and cosmos.

The more you relax your body, breathe deeply, and enjoy the sensual pleasures of being alive, the more you attune to, and welcome in, these auspicious gifts.

SECRETS

The mystical, all-seeing coin produces a single drop of *rubedo* — the red alchemical substance that merges all aspects of the self with the Divine, creating spiritual gold, and allowing you to embody your highest potential and most effective level of being.

To the right of the coin, we see the symbol for Jupiter and tin. Jupiter is the planet of expansion and the god of luck, and tin is the metal associated with both.

In the upper right corner, we see the symbol for the earth element, which is also represented by the rabbit, the magical exemplification and conscious aliveness of the earth element, who is nestled safely in the lush grass studded with wild daisies. Rabbits, like daisies, grass, and Jupiter, are magical expressions of expansion, multiplication, and luck.

MEANINGS AND MESSAGES OF ACE OF COINS:

- Luck is on your side.
- Money is coming to you.
- A financial opportunity will be successful.
- Positive conditions are expanding.

- Your wealth is multiplying.
- Keep going; you are on the right track.
- Whatever you are asking about will be a success.
- Relax and enjoy, through your senses, all that you already have, and even more blessings will come to you.
- Your inner and outer work has paid off, and you are now poised to reap fabulous rewards.

MEANINGS AND MESSAGES OF ACE OF COINS — REVERSED:

- Luck is trying to find you, but you are holding it at bay with your fear or sense of unworthiness. Relax, trust, and cultivate a sense of ease.
- Money will flow to you once you let go of fears or limiting beliefs.
- There is another step you need to take before a financial opportunity will yield success. Light a candle, relax, and ask for divine messages about how to change your mindset and proceed.
- Positive conditions will expand for you, but first you must believe and allow yourself to receive.
- If your wealth is diminishing, you can easily turn this around. Align with the earth, attune to your senses, and set the intention to attract money and success.
- Stop for just a moment and take some time to get your finances in order. Help is here for you, but you must look clearly at what you have and how you can make wise decisions.

- More information is needed. Whatever you are asking about can be a success once you get clear on what you are working with and responsibly choose how to proceed.
- Remember to enjoy what you already have. Pay attention to sensory pleasures and cultivate an attitude of gratitude, and you will begin to naturally magnetize even more to enjoy and be grateful for.
- Align your inner beliefs with your outer goals and you will establish the resonance that will naturally manifest your desires.

TWO OF COINS

INTENTION PLUS ACTION

GUIDANCE

Enter into a transaction or negotiation to expand your world and stimulate personal growth. Challenge yourself to invest in your future and to obtain a greater level of financial mastery. Become even more affluent — don't settle for the status quo.

Where you are in life might be lovely, but if you don't have something new to aim for and look forward to, you will begin to get bored and to take your blessings for granted. Take a risk and reach for something better. To triumph, draw upon your own wisdom and enlist the help of others you respect. Retaining wealth requires responsibility, so commit to being a conscientious steward of your affairs.

You may fear that when you apply yourself to taking care of your finances and affairs, you will become overwhelmed. Perhaps you worry that you will become a stick-in-the-mud who never behaves spontaneously or has any fun. In fact, financial responsibility empowers you. It helps you to become more liberated, not less. Once you begin to get the hang of it, it doesn't weigh on you but lifts you up.

If you expect it to be, you will find that money mindfulness is fun. It is a fabulous adventure towards an ever-increasing sense of worthiness and worth.

DYNAMICS

The polarity between eagle and lion mirrors the polarity of the coins. Duality creates useful tension. It is a dynamic relationship of giving, receiving, and creating something new. To be a responsible steward of wealth and resources, we must be active and awake; not remaining solitary in our work, but actively employing the support and wisdom of others and the physical world.

Earthly existence is not separate from spiritual existence. Mastering one can help you master the other. Approach one with mindfulness, and it will inform how you bring mindfulness to the other. Don't discount your financial and physical well-being out of a false belief that such things are pedantic or woefully mundane.

SECRETS

The resting eagle is latent volatility. The leaping lion is active fixation. Linked together with a vital cord of alchemical *rubedo* (the alchemical red fluid that aids transmutation), each stokes the other, allowing for perpetual motion in the realms of creation, expansion, and success.

Hovering in the ether, we see symbols for mercury, sulfur, and salt, the materials that combine in various forms to actively form all that we experience and see. In the upper right corner, we see the symbol for earth.

Remember to look for what you have to work with, and to be an active participant in creating, amassing, and retaining your fortune. You are qualified. You have more resources than you think you do. Invoke divine help, jump into the action, and learn by doing.

MEANINGS AND MESSAGES OF TWO OF COINS:

- Take action on expanding your wealth.
- Take a calculated risk.
- Proactively get your finances and affairs in order.
- Invest in your future.
- Get in the habit of managing your money well.
- Work with what you have to expand into new levels of success.
- Follow your intuition to expand your wealth, and learn as you go.
- A seeming challenge will work to your benefit.

MEANINGS AND MESSAGES OF TWO OF COINS — REVERSED:

- Bust out of a rut by taking bold action.
- Stop hesitating. Be bold and try something new in the realm of wealth and finances.
- Ignoring financial problems won't make them go away. But a clear intention coupled with decisive action will.
- See your options through fresh eyes. There is more potential here than you realize.
- Decide to manage your finances responsibly. Then do it.
- Stop believing that you don't have options. You do.
- Don't be afraid to make mistakes.
- You are perceiving yourself as less well off than you are, and it's keeping you stuck. Look with fresh eyes and try a new approach.

THREE OF COINS

APPLICATION MEETS COLLABORATION

GUIDANCE

Your diligent efforts are about to pay off. Collaboration builds structure and fuels progress. Focus, work hard, and strategically enlist help and you will succeed.

You are building something tangible, lasting, and of great value. By applying yourself, utilizing all your resources, and being humble enough to ask for help, you are positioning yourself for great and enduring success.

You have the talent, focus, and drive. Others may have the money, resources, and connections. Value the work and let its unfolding inform what you do. Seek out and request the assistance you need, even if it feels vulnerable to reveal that you want something that others have.

Be patient. Adopt a pace that is steady, persistent, and controlled. Don't pester. Trust in divine timing and wait for others to respond in their own time and way.

DYNAMICS

Three legs on a stool make it sturdy. Three ropes in a braid make it strong. Three primary colors combine to create a rainbow.

In a numerical creation story, Primordial Oneness cleaves into two: the Goddess and the God. From these two, three is born: from three comes everything — all that we can measure and see.

Similarly, your vision or goal is epic, and requires more than two participants, though no two contributors will perform the same function. You may have the vision and the work ethic, while others will offer some form of specialized help, wisdom, or expertise.

SECRETS

A sturdy house is a positive limitation: the walls and roof keep the elements out and wealth in. It is also a lasting and collaborative project — something that spans consecutive human lifetimes and takes time and teamwork to create, improve, and maintain.

Below the home is the glowing core of the earth. Above it is a sphere that represents the infinite light of the cosmos. Within, then, there is a masterful mix of grounding and inspiration. Over time, slowly, surely, and methodically, earth magic, cosmic energy, and generational contributions coalesce to build a strong geometrical structure of light. With loving help from residents, mystics, benefactors, designers, gardeners, architects, artists, and artisans, the home's past, present, and future care team collaborates to feed the structure's sentience and shore up its power.

MEANINGS AND MESSAGES OF THREE OF COINS:

- You are a master at what you do, or you have gained a degree of mastery that is allowing you to create the conditions you desire. Now let that mastery shine by enlisting experts to help you in areas that are other than your own.
- Stay true to your vision and carry it out with persistence and humility, asking for help as needed and waiting patiently for that help to come through.
- Be willing to collaborate and get curious about how teamwork can make your creation or vision even better than before.
- Acknowledge your team and express gratitude for the diverse talents and gifts each collaborator brings to the table.
- If you believe, expect, and act as if everyone wants you to succeed, you *will* succeed.
- Receiving support for your vision is a privilege and a sign of success.

MEANINGS AND MESSAGES OF THREE OF COINS — REVERSED:

- Change the paradigm that you need to control everything or do it all on your own.

- Don't rush and don't be too proud to ask for help. Be willing to wait and be willing to open yourself up to failure, rejection, or disappointment.
- If you ask for help and the answer is no, or if you receive that help and it's not what you had hoped, you can always ask someone else or try again.
- Don't hoard the limelight. Receive credit according to your due, but let the project take precedence over your ego.
- If you believe, expect, and act as if everyone wants you to fail, you are heading for failure. But you can turn this around.
- After asking for help, be willing to incorporate the wishes and visions of others.

FOUR OF COINS

BURIED WEALTH

GUIDANCE

Recalibrate your relationship with money and resources. Wasting money and resources is not wise, but neither is hoarding such things for their own sake. Wealth is not static — it is a dynamic form of energy that requires clarity and respect.

Be an astute custodian of your finances rather than inadvertently placing yourself in their thrall. Wealth, when feared or hoarded, becomes your controller. But when you utilize it, invest it, grow it, and courageously allow it to flow to you and through you, you have recognized its magic, and you have stepped into your rightful role as its boss.

Patience is a virtue, but so is jumping on an opportunity as you feel guided, even when that opportunity contains an element of risk. Adopt an adventurous sense of play around money. Set clear intentions related to how you would like to earn it, save it, invest it, spend it, and receive benefits from it. Once you have tuned yourself into the frequency of your prosperity-related intentions, listen to and feel the nudges of the universe. Then act.

DYNAMICS

A financial decision or deal has been temporarily paused, or you are relating to your finances in a way that restricts positive movement and flow. Remember that wealth is more than just a number on your bank statement. It also includes your assets, your investments, your happiness, your health, the people and experiences that are priceless to you, and your perceived degree of luxury and affluence.

This is a message to both expand your view of wealth, and to get things moving financially in some significant way.

Place your awareness on all the ways you are already lucky and rich, so you can begin to vibrate at the frequency of lavish abundance.

Accept that all financial dealings contain an element of risk.

Be wise in your actions, but do not overly value the status quo to the point of stagnation, for wealth wants to flow. When you invest it wisely and with joy, it comes back to you multiplied. But not always in the ways you might have wished for or expected.

SECRETS

Four coins have been buried in the soil and hidden away from the world. The shaman senses their presence and is performing magic over them, so that they can stop lying dormant and begin, like seeds, to sprout and then grow. In time, with his magical assistance, they will multiply exponentially, bringing great and enduring wealth to many.

In the upper right, we see the sign for Jupiter and tin, the planet and metal of growth, generosity, and expansion.

MEANINGS AND MESSAGES OF FOUR OF COINS:

- Be brave and invest your money in something that will help it to grow.
- Don't worry if your financial dealings are not perfect in every way. Just do your best with what you have and with how the market is now.
- If someone is asking for a donation, investment, or loan, consider giving it to them.
- If your intuition is nudging you to invest in schooling, housing, the stock market, or some kind of business, follow it.
- Expand your paradigm of wealth to include more than just a number: remember assets, investments, and everyday blessings as well.

MEANINGS AND MESSAGES OF FOUR OF COINS — REVERSED:

- Hoarding money out of fear is keeping you financially stuck.
- When it comes to investing, conditions will never be exactly perfect in every way, but when you flow with divine guidance and trust in your divine supply, every condition can be a blessing, even if that blessing is temporarily disguised.

- What you send out returns to you multiplied. Giving generously and with an open heart will present the opportunity, in time, to receive.
- Your intuition is nudging you to act, but you are overriding that nudge, which is causing your finances to stagnate.
- By overidentifying with the number in your checking or savings account, you are missing out on present moment abundance and letting opportunities pass you by.

FIVE OF COINS

CHANGE THE NARRATIVE

GUIDANCE

You feel as if you are destitute, excluded, or alone, but this isn't true. You may have less money and fewer resources than you had imagined or hoped for, but this is only temporary. Take a deep breath and relax — help is already on the way.

The biggest hazard you currently face is not lack but worry. It's not rejection but the sense that you don't belong. It's not an unfriendly world, but the uneasy suspicion that is a defensive response to loneliness. In other words, you are temporarily in the grip of fear, and you are mistaking for truth the illusions produced by a fearful mind.

Steady your mind and reframe your perspective. Breathe, relax, take care of yourself, and expand your expectation of what's possible. The solution is here for you. When you face it bravely, the challenge will prove to be far easier than you previously believed.

You may need to ask for advice, think creatively, and seek out an unexpected solution to your problem. But giving up before you try is the only way to ensure that you will fail.

DYNAMICS

When we are tired, we fail to be as empathetic as we would otherwise be, and we become suspicious. When we are lonely, we expect the outside world to be hostile, and so we isolate ourselves even more. But we can turn such dynamics around by resting, meditating, taking care of ourselves, reaching out to others, and choosing to believe and perceive in fresh and more positive ways.

Meditate, spend time in nature, and count the many blessings you already have. Remember the kindnesses you have received from others, and the kindnesses you have performed on others' behalf. Laugh and smile. Breathe the fresh air and feel the sunlight on your skin. Soak in the love and support of nature, the universe, and your fellow earthlings. Rediscover your intrinsic sense of belonging and your natural flow of wealth.

SECRETS

Cosmic hands tie a red string in a neat bow, illustrating that even in your seeming isolation, Spirit watches over you, protecting you, blessing you, and wishing you well.

Though it is temporarily invisible to you, a coin of fortune hovers above you, and four hover beneath you. You are beloved by Spirit and an heir to the lavish abundance of the universe. Divine guidance is here for you. Lucky breaks hover in the ether, merely awaiting your recognition.

The alchemical symbol for tin and Jupiter hints at the expansion that is yours, just as soon as you are ready to claim it.

MEANINGS AND MESSAGES OF FIVE OF COINS:

- Turn worry around.
- Clear and revise limiting beliefs about money, resources, and love.
- Take care of yourself lovingly to support positive new perspectives.
- Cultivate self-love, self-approval, and an expectation that you will thrive.
- Ask for help, expect help, and proactively turn your luck around.
- This is just a temporary struggle or setback. Rest and regroup as needed but rise to the challenge and don't give up.

MEANINGS AND MESSAGES OF FIVE OF COINS — REVERSED:

- A challenge is a blessing in disguise, as it is alerting you to a harmful habit or an erroneous assumption.
- Your worry is causing you to see things as being scarier or more threatening than they are.

- You are acting out of fear, which is creating more problems than it solves. As soon as you acknowledge this, you can turn it around.
- Change the habit of negative self-talk. Begin to speak to yourself in positive and helpful ways.
- Just because you've experienced challenges in the past, that doesn't mean you will continue to experience the same challenges in the future.
- Occasional problems are not punishment or proof that you are unworthy — they are inevitable features of the human experience. Change your story, be compassionate with yourself, and let go of any inner narratives that keep you stuck.

SIX OF COINS
CHARITY IN FLOW

GUIDANCE

Financial support is here for you. The resources you need are available or on their way. Receive fully and give as you are guided, and you will uncover an intrinsic sense of stability, safety, and well-being.

There's no need to worry about money or physical resources, as you are a beloved child of Spirit, and Spirit provides.

Perhaps, however, you may need to expand your willingness to ask for and accept gifts, loans, grants, and other forms of charity and largesse.

Or, depending on the situation, this may be a message to give a gift, repay a loan, or sponsor someone in need.

DYNAMICS

Independence is an overrated virtue, and an illusion besides. As children, we are all dependent on adults. And when we are grown, our well-being is interwoven with the well-being of others, and with the highest and truest good of all.

Remember, too, that just like you do, most people enjoy helping and being of service when they can. So, in receiving a gift, you are also offering one.

Let others be agents of Spirit, as they lovingly provide you with the funds and supplies you need. Or, be such an agent of Spirit yourself.

You need not be perfect to be worthy of blessings, gifts, and miraculous windfalls. None of us are. You need not seek to make yourself worthy, for the Divine sees your intrinsic worthiness regardless of what you do.

You need only feel grateful as you accept the gifts that are offered. Let them open your heart and inspire you, in turn, to naturally offer support to others when you feel guided, and when you have the means.

S E C R E T S

This child was an orphan, dressed in rags, and now she holds out her arms to inspect the finery in which she has been clothed.

With the sun before her and the lush grass beneath her feet, she is warm, safe, and held comfortably by the earth.

After a warm bath, her hair has been gently combed and styled by her loving caregiver.

The owl on her head symbolizes her wisdom in deftly rearranging her expectations to meet her newfound affluence. Where once she expected poverty, now she realizes she can expect to have everything she wants and needs, and more.

The six coins hover before her, as they will continue to do throughout her life, as she knows in her innermost core that she will always be a child of fortune. In allowing herself to receive charity and love, she has attuned herself to the frequency of wealth.

And, when she grows up, when others are in need, she will be especially inclined to give as she is able.

MEANINGS AND MESSAGES OF SIX OF COINS:

- Spirit and helpful people are offering you support. Receive it.
- Apply for a loan, request a favor, or be humble enough to ask for what you need.
- Expect a miraculous windfall, and when you receive it, feel and express gratitude.
- There is wisdom in both giving and receiving.
- You can be grateful without feeling unworthy. You can give back without feeling woefully indebted.
- Generosity is not a one-way street but an endless mandala of light.
- Upgrade your expectations and know that you deserve to thrive.

MEANINGS AND MESSAGES OF SIX OF COINS – REVERSED:

- Support is here for you, but you must allow yourself to receive it. Relax, breathe, and ask Spirit for help with this.
- If you are too proud to ask for what you need, no one will know how to help.

- Don't expect to fail. Remember that success is possible and shift your sense of what is probable.
- Refusing to give or receive help is keeping you stuck.
- You don't need to earn worthiness or love, just as others don't need to be perfect in order to be deserving of your support.
- Simply ask for what you need. Then, trust others to respond honestly about what they desire to give.
- Let go of negative beliefs about deservedness and indebtedness.

SEVEN OF COINS

HONEST WORK

GUIDANCE

You have been working with conscientious persistence, and it's starting to pay off. Or such an approach is just what you need to succeed. Either way, methodical diligence will earn you wealth and get you from where you are to where you want to be.

Work hard, work smart, and commit for the long haul. Over time, if you adopt this habit and dutifully show up again and again to accomplish your daily tasks, you will surely thrive.

While success or abundance may not come as quickly or as thoroughly as you had hoped, dogged persistence will eventually get you where you want to go. The secret is to attend to the journey, rather than being dazzled by the promise of the prize.

DYNAMICS

One brick at a time builds the tower.

In other words, reaching a treasured goal requires many little steps. If you become overwhelmed by thinking about all of them at once, you may discourage yourself from beginning or continuing along your path. But if, instead, you think about showing up day after day to do what you can do with what you have, in time, you will succeed.

And, in the process, you will find joy. For life is not about finish lines, but about the ongoing experience of being. While relaxation is certainly an important factor in our wellness, the fact remains that we're built for hard work. When we're in divine flow—in other words when we "get into a zone"—we merge with the moment and feel at peace with ourselves and the world.

The mastery is in having the goal, but committing not just to the goal, but also to the entire process of getting from here to there. This is where true happiness dwells.

While there are many little successes and stopping points along the way, one's life work is never quite finished. For if you are still alive, there is still more to do.

SECRETS

This is a tower made of the liminal and limitless. By working with the finite stuff this physical existence—the planets, elements, and the minerals of the earth—you find infinity. You start with mundane lead and tap into spiritual gold. Or you start with spiritual gold and discover that lead had contained everything you needed all along.

Your work is the catalyst. Your work brings sustenance, but it also leads you to supreme joy, profound satisfaction, and present-moment peace.

MEANINGS AND MESSAGES OF SEVEN OF COINS:

- Slow, methodical work will win the day.
- You have been working hard and it's paying off. Keep at it.
- Hard work will bring you success.
- Hard work will help your existing success to persist and expand.
- Earn wealth through working hard and expending your energy wisely.
- Proactively look for opportunities to work.
- Find joy in mundane tasks and the everyday business of living.
- Be conscientious and diligent, and work your way up.

MEANINGS AND MESSAGES OF SEVEN OF COINS — REVERSED:

- Don't try to do it all at once or get overwhelmed by all the steps. Instead, begin. Then, using practical steps and methodical habits, continue.

- Don't cut corners or expect a big break to come out of nowhere. Be responsible and be willing to work hard for as long as it takes.
- Be patient and responsible. Nurture your success with positive work habits.
- The solution to your problem involves hard work.
- You are waiting around for something to change when you should be out working hard and creating your own luck.
- Restructure your values and choose to find joy in being in the flow of your day-to-day tasks.
- Don't shy away from honest work. Start at the bottom if you need to and work your way up.

EIGHT OF COINS

EIGHT OF COINS

MOMENTUM

GUIDANCE

It's all happening. Your hard work has led to mastery, which in turn is bringing some well-deserved success. Your finances are growing, and your accomplishments are increasing.

While at first your effort may have felt like an uphill slog, you've established a momentum, which is making it easier for you to continue. You had raw talent before, but now you have skill, and you find satisfaction in proficiency.

While you may have seen a lucky break or two along the way, you also showed up on your own behalf. You met that help halfway by doing everything you could on your end. Now, you are seeing the benefits of your honest work.

DYNAMICS

The novice alchemist senses that earthly elements and the subtle realm hold great potential for magic, but she doesn't yet know how to manipulate them to transform her world in accordance with her will. Over time, she studies and practices the art of magic until one day, it becomes like second nature to her. She and her discipline are one. On that day, she is a master.

Similarly, in some important life area, you are now coming into your own. In spirituality, work, life, or art, you have become incredibly capable. Step into your greatness and embody your ability to manifest and succeed. Your craft feels far easier to you now, not because it is easy, but because you have painstakingly shown up for the regular practice required to make it easy for *you*.

Such mastery benefits you, certainly. Additionally, it benefits other people and the world.

S E C R E T S

On this palm, we see the symbol for tin and the planet Jupiter. Jupiter is the old man, Jove: the wise mage who can hear the intelligence of the earth, harness the magic of the stars, and combine invisible elements and base metals to create sparkling spiritual gold.

By putting all the coins of focused intelligence in order, the top coin connects with Spirit, drawing down and synchronizing your actions with divine orchestration and cosmic guidance.

MEANINGS AND MESSAGES OF EIGHT OF COINS:

- Acknowledge yourself for your honest work and continue to show up to your daily tasks so you can keep this positive momentum on track.
- Become conscious of the ways your work habits have changed once difficult tasks into easy ones and enjoy exercising the feeling of mastery in your chosen discipline or craft.
- You have unlocked your own potential, and you are now reaping the rewards of your positive habits.
- Enjoy exercising the skill you have achieved. Devote your work toward positive and constructive aims.
- What may appear to the world as rapid progress or overnight success is, in truth, the result of long-term effort you have put toward a chosen discipline or goal.

MEANINGS AND MESSAGES OF EIGHT OF COINS — REVERSED:

- Stick to a project or endeavor for just a little longer. Take a break to recharge if you need to, but then come back and keep going.
- It may feel like you are not making progress, but you are. Keep going and divine momentum will soon flow in to carry you through.
- Don't let one lapse discourage you. Everyone stumbles now and again. The secret is to simply stand up, dust yourself off, and keep going.

- You have even more wisdom and experience than you think you do. Trust, believe, and access the mastery you have earned.
- Remember that overnight success only looks that way in the eyes of the world. In fact, it requires months, years, or even decades of effort that appear to have little or no effect, until, one day, your momentum is established, and your divine success begins to visibly flow.

NINE OF COINS

HARNESSED WEALTH

GUIDANCE

Your hard work is paying off. Relax and enjoy the marvelous world you have created for yourself to live in. Gratefully acknowledge the incredible magic you have harnessed to manifest such luxury and ease.

After showing up for yourself and your goal again and again, through the good times and the lean ones, you have triumphed many times over, and you have attracted incredible inner success or outer prosperity.

Wear beautiful clothes. Eat delicious food. Bask in sunlight on a gorgeous beach. Take some time to delight in the spiritual joy that shines through the material luxury you have amassed.

Pace yourself as you take joy in the process of getting even wealthier and managing the beautiful conditions you've already established.

DYNAMICS

Imagine a glorious grove of oak trees, and all the stages the trees have gone through since they were saplings. They have seen all the seasons. The wind has ravaged them. The thunder has frightened them. The lightning has threatened to strike them down before their prime.

But now they are secure in their existence. They are resting in the sunlight and the gentle breeze, letting their leaves sparkle and their branches dance.

In addition to the material wealth and physical beauty you have accumulated, you have evolved spiritually along the way. Through your focused diligence, you have begun with tin and turned it to gold.

SECRETS

You grew these oak trees from acorns. You seeded this turf, and weeded it, and mowed it faithfully. You prepared the land in the distance for planting, and sowed season after season of prosperous crops, as you perfected your strategy and technique.

You harnessed the magic of the earth with the red thread of magical mastery and channeled it intently toward manifesting your desires and goals.

Now, you can stop for a moment and say to yourself, "I built this, through alchemy and prolonged practical effort. I called on the Divine and magical principles, and it worked. Thank you, self. Thank you, Earth. Thank you, universe."

MEANINGS AND MESSAGES OF NINE OF COINS:

- Dwell in the luxury you have established and enjoy the wealth you've earned.
- Congratulate yourself: you did it.
- You had a vision. You worked toward it, and now it is here.
- Smile and appreciate the world you have built within and around yourself.
- Enjoy your senses and sensory pleasures.
- Your wealth is expanding.
- Just look at all the magic you've brought forth. You did this! You created this. You should be proud.
- Your hard work is paying off and your orchards are coming to fruition. Relax and enjoy.

MEANINGS AND MESSAGES OF NINE OF COINS — REVERSED:

- You've established luxury and earned wealth, but you're not letting yourself enjoy or appreciate it.
- Before you move onto the next project that needs to be tackled, be sure to appreciate the fruits of your labor thus far.
- Now that you've manifested a goal, you are feeling intimidated by the responsibility you hold.
- Dare to trust that you are ready to manage the world you have built and the success you have unlocked.
- Get out of your head and into your body so you can appreciate all that you've established and all that you already have.

- Your wealth is expanding, so be sure to relax and recharge so you can manage it well.
- You are a beloved child of the Divine. Relax your body and conjure up a sense of deep inner knowing that you deserve the beautiful gifts the universe has helped you bring forth.
- When you relax and enjoy all that you already have, you will receive clear and reliable guidance about how to manage your wealth and continually expand it.

TEN OF COINS

CONTINUUM OF WEALTH

GUIDANCE

Material abundance is yours in a lasting way. You have succeeded, and you will continue to succeed. You are operating from a solid base and have access to an endless support system of helpful people, physical resources, and spiritual sustenance.

Through a combination of luck, diligent effort, and wise choices, you are tapped into a continuum of wealth.

Relax and enjoy, even as you continue to listen to your intuition, tend to your bounty, and bring forth even more prosperity.

DYNAMICS

This is the victorious conclusion without end — the fruit tree that continually produces, the business that keeps expanding, and the investment that keeps paying off.

You are in a groove. You've found your way. You have honored the ancestors and contributed to your community, and now seen and unseen teams of helpers are guiding and providing for you in turn.

You are a part of everything, and everything contributes to your prospering. Your physical and financial well-being is inextricably intertwined with that of your friends, neighbors, family, community, and world.

SECRETS

Within a waning moon, the symbol for Jupiter hovers. Positioned between the full moon (above) and the dark moon (below), we see a woman in the second half of her life. This is middle to older age, when youth is gone but wisdom is anchored in the Infinite, and wealth is on a trajectory of limitless growth.

She is a living treasure, with brimming repositories and a profound generosity of spirit. Her wealth overflows and blesses those in her orbit. As she cares for her elders and the younger generations, she gathers blessings from them in turn. There is sparkling silver intertwined with her hair, and ten gold coins hover brightly in her wake.

In giving, she receives. In receiving, she offers a gift.

She knows that while she has made wise decisions and stayed focused on her goals, she has not done so singlehandedly. A village has backed her and will back her still, for she is a vital component of its thriving.

She recognizes her privileges but does not eschew them. This is true wisdom and the ability to amass affluence without getting tripped up by the ego's desire to take all the credit for one's success.

MEANINGS AND MESSAGES OF TEN OF COINS:

- Great wealth is here for you.
- You are coming into money.
- You have access to lasting and sustainable resources.
- You have a solid support system that will help you continue to thrive.
- Through wise choices and hard work, you have achieved long-term financial success.
- You learned the principles of lasting success, and you applied them.
- You have set yourself up for ever-increasing success.
- A momentum of expansion has been achieved.
- You have painstakingly built an empire that will last.

MEANINGS AND MESSAGES OF TEN OF COINS — REVERSED:

- Great wealth is here for you, but you must accept and allow it.
- You are feeling guilty about receiving.
- By believing that you must do everything yourself, you are resisting the wealth that could otherwise flow.
- Support others and they will support you back. This will help everyone to thrive.
- You are ready for this successful next phase, but you must first accept and believe that this is so.

- Ask for help and receive it. This will open you up to the success and wealth you seek.
- See your success as connected to everyone else's success, and you will open up to greater wealth and personal fulfillment.
- Expand your view and timeline so that your goal will not terminate when you reach it but will continue to expand and gain momentum over time.
- Don't focus on the short-term conclusion, but instead build an empire that will last.

PRINCESS OF COINS

PRACTICAL DREAMER

GUIDANCE

This is a young student, healer, artist, or entrepreneur, or a person of any age newly embarking upon a practical avenue of discipline, work, or financial investment. There may be a forthcoming message about money or resources. Or a sensual new era of wealth and luxury is about to bloom.

Revel in your senses. Inhabit your body. Ground yourself in the physical world. Identify where the Princess of Coins is showing up in this situation and take note of how she plays a part.

DYNAMICS

While many students, neophytes, and adolescents are dreamy and starry-eyed, or enthusiastic but unreliable, not so for the Princess of Coins. She is steady, realistic, and dependable to a fault. While she can easily adapt as needed, she cannot be shaken or swayed.

When inspiration is anchored in pragmatism, your goal is on the slow-and-steady track to victory. In your commitment to humble, incremental progress, you will not be easily dissuaded or thrown off course.

Whether the Princess of Coins represents you or someone else, she is a helpful ally: wise in the ways of earth wisdom, natural healing, and lasting financial well-being.

S E C R E T S

Crowned with variegated poppies and with a necklace made from one red bloom and mystical red thread, her bare feet are planted firmly on the fertile earth. Luxurious fabric adorns her like a weighted blanket, anchoring her in her body and filling her with present moment peace. Young as well as young at heart, her gaze is not, appearing both ancient and wise.

Rubedo is the red liquid on the left. *Albedo* is the white liquid on the right. The coin brings life. The waning moon brings death. Decay makes for fertile soil which in turn grows an abundant crop. On the border of such fertile change, the Princess of Coins works with what's happening, adapting any condition to serve her aim.

MEANINGS AND MESSAGES OF PRINCESS OF COINS:

- A young or youthful student, healer, artist, or entrepreneur appears in this situation.
- You are embarking on a new discipline or financial venture.
- Expect news about healing, resources, or money.
- You are grounded in practicality.
- You are enlisting the help of a natural healer or drawing upon your own ability to heal with the wisdom of the earth.
- You are focused on your goal or project for the long haul.
- As you embark on a new journey or project, your perseverance, practicality, and adaptability will serve you well.
- You are joining or invited to join a school or group focused on earth healing, finances, or physical resources.
- You are an initiate of an earth-based discipline, or an area of study related to physical resources and wealth.

MEANINGS AND MESSAGES OF PRINCESS OF COINS — REVERSED:

- A formerly focused student, healer, artist, or entrepreneur (possibly you) is now questioning the initial commitment.
- You are seeing a project or journey in a new light, which requires you to either abandon or rethink it.
- News about money, healing, or resources is delayed or not what you hoped.

- Come back to the present moment and take stock of your day-to-day concerns.
- A natural healer or your own healing efforts did not deliver as you had wished.
- Something has distracted you from your vision. Bring yourself back and adapt to new circumstances as needed.
- Sometimes it's okay to let something go. You can keep your values while releasing what is no longer working (or never worked the way you had anticipated).
- Get honest about toxic dynamics in a school or group related to earth healing, finances, or physical resources.
- You've outgrown a teacher, discipline, or study program, or you've discovered it isn't what you thought it was. Leave or distance yourself as appropriate.

KNIGHT OF COINS

ELEGANT INVESTOR

GUIDANCE

This is an elegant person in their 20s or 30s who is wise in the ways of wealth, or an investor or businessperson of any age who knows that patience and methodical hard work will always, eventually, yield positive results. Long-term affluence carries special significance. Attend to your finances, cultivate chic minimalism, and make wise monetary choices.

This is not a time for sudden moves, but a time to look at the big picture and build sustainable avenues of wealth. Tend to tangible well-being of all varieties, including in the realms of health, home, community, and investments.

Whether the Knight of Coins signifies you or someone else, be aware of their presence in this situation and the level-headed prudence that provides a solid framework and foundation for success.

DYNAMICS

While the Knight of Coins is more than capable when swift action is needed, they do not, by their nature, rush ahead. Instead, with calm logic and cool self-mastery, they protect and nurture their fortune and feel deep satisfaction as they watch it grow.

But make no mistake: while patient, they are not lazy. They work slowly, but tirelessly, and over time, their incremental toil adds up.

While such focused diligence yields incredible wealth, the Knight of Coins is not a slave to trends and abhors clutter. They prefer a few high-end and long-lasting pieces to chintzy baubles and quickly passing fads.

While in the short term, acquiring high-quality goods may seem like an extravagance, over time, the Knight of Coins knows that valuing quality over quantity is the savvier path. Particularly when one's tastes are classic and timeless, weathering fashion's whims and transcending the capricious styles of the day.

SECRETS

The symbol for the abundant planet of Jupiter hovers beneath the knight's right hand, illustrating that focus will yield expansion.

The dark moon hovers below the knight's left hand, symbolizing receptivity and a willingness to enjoy. One may work hard and amass great wealth, but without self-esteem and a sense of deservingness, there will be poverty of the soul.

The knight's castle is behind them. All around them is their fertile realm, and some of their bounty is amassed at their feet.

Much like the knight, the horse is calm, but perfectly poised for action whenever needed.

MEANINGS AND MESSAGES OF KNIGHT OF COINS:

- Look for the calm businessperson or wise investor in this situation. This might be you.
- Don't make sudden moves. Choose a practical approach and take it one step at a time.
- Build a strong foundation.
- Cultivate sustainable avenues of income.
- Patiently tend to your health and physical well-being.
- Get your finances in order.
- Cultivate elegant minimalism and focus on quality over quantity.
- Once you look at all the angles and patiently gather wisdom with the clearest of minds, proceed.

MEANINGS AND MESSAGES OF KNIGHT OF COINS – REVERSED:

- Someone in this situation (maybe you) will benefit from cultivating patience and placing attention on long-term goals.
- It may be tempting to move forward immediately, but don't. This is a time to be patient and to take a practical approach.
- The foundation isn't there yet. Get that in place before you rush ahead.
- Even though something may yield dazzling results in the short term, there's a longer-term option that will be even more lucrative.
- Don't ignore your physical health and material needs.
- Get clear on what you have and create new structures and strategies with regards to your finances.
- Restructure your values to place an emphasis on minimalism and quality rather than flashy and external measures of status.
- Don't assume you know everything without doing your due diligence. Take your time and get the whole story before you proceed.

QUEEN OF COINS

MATRIARCH OF THE EARTH'S RICHES

GUIDANCE

Here is a prosperous, earthy, caring person at middle age or older, or a loving and financially savvy matriarch-type of any age. Make wise business choices and tend to physical-world concerns. Establish and hold space for elegance, comfort, and a perpetual increase of wealth.

Align with the healing vibrations of the earth. Inhabit your body and revel in your senses. Attune to divine rhythm and let your grounded presence inform your next move.

Be a queenly, masterful, and motherly authority or acknowledge someone else who is presently embodying such a role.

DYNAMICS

The Queen of Coins draws upon her body's inner knowing and her close alignment with the fertile wisdom of the earth.

She may grow beautiful flowers and healthful foods in her garden and share them. She may prepare medicines for herself and others with fruits, vegetables, and herbs. Or she may provide sustenance, housing, and healing through her career, business, or investments.

She prioritizes her own nourishment and the nourishment of those in her family, community, and circle.

This queen sees no separation between mysticism and business, spirituality and the material world. In truth, they are two sides of one coin. When we attend to both, we thrive.

The Queen of Coins places her attention on fertile possibilities and makes beautiful things grow.

SECRETS

This queen is so rooted into the earth, a profusion of grasses and grain grow out of her crown chakra, extending up and out into the sky.

Much like the sun, she shines her light generously, warming hearts and causing plants to flourish.

Her hair is made of starlight, for she knows that within the physical realm, magic lives. The infinite shines through the finite. Sensual pleasure aligns us with spirit, healing us and making us whole.

The symbol for tin and Jupiter hovers above her in the ether, for wherever she goes, abundance grows.

MEANINGS AND MESSAGES OF QUEEN OF COINS:

- A practical and prosperous queen-like figure has appeared in this situation.
- Tend to your finances and make wise business choices.
- Take care of your body, home, and physical space.
- Fertility is present — something is gestating or about to be born.
- Eat intuitively and care for your body with delicious and wholesome foods.
- Make choices that will help you provide for your family and loved ones.
- Look for possibilities to expand your finances, business, or career.
- Get grounded, attune to your body's innate wisdom and receive the supportive energy of the earth.

MEANINGS AND MESSAGES OF QUEEN OF COINS — REVERSED:

- Someone in this situation (maybe you) is so concerned about finances, health issues, or other physical world concerns, they have forgotten to attend to their body's clear inner knowing about the best route to take.

- Stop, regroup, and rearrange your priorities. Start with nurturing, presence, and love.
- You will naturally make the wisest choices and reap the most rewards when you ground and center your energy and recalibrate with the magic and wisdom of the earth.
- Something wants to be born, but first you must ground your energy, clarify your intentions, and create the space.
- You have temporarily strayed from your body's innate inner wisdom about what will nourish you best, perhaps because of overwhelm, diet culture, deprivation, food insecurity, or external and false ideas about health or beauty. But you can heal this when you stop listening to everyone else and listen to yourself.
- You are qualified to be a competent leader and provider, but you need to trust yourself.
- Stop disbelieving in your ability to succeed. Take calculated risks to expand.
- Clear clutter from your schedule and physical space so you can rest, focus, and come back into harmony with your body and the earth.

KING OF COINS

KING OF COINS
STEADFAST PROVIDER

G U I D A N C E

The King of Coins is a protective, financially stable, head-of-household type of middle age or older, or a conscientious leader or fatherly person of any age. Tend to your finances, establish a sturdy home base for yourself and others, and provide for those you love. Be a grounded, solid, and durable bastion of support.

Keep your eyes on your finances and your incremental path to financial longevity and increase. Weed out attachment to outer indications of status. Be the leader who delights in helping others succeed.

True elegance is almost invisible, for its aesthetic is like that of the earth: a subtle ecosystem of harmonious beauty and authentic depth, content with its simplicity; humble in its complexity.

DYNAMICS

This king is incredibly focused, practical, and reliable. In fact, he is so steadfast, some of those in his orbit don't even realize how much comfort they draw from his presence. In this way, he is like the earth and the natural world: everything to us, and too often taken for granted.

He is the father who saves money not because he has little, but because he prioritizes his family, loathes waste, and has no interest in excess. Never one to fritter funds or wastefully accumulate, he takes the time to find just the right items only when he needs them, because he prefers to have a minimal number of high-quality belongings that last.

He will drive a well-made car for decades while keeping it in fabulous shape, cherish a gold watch that has been in the family for generations, and wear the same pair of comfortable Italian loafers until they just can't be repaired one more time.

All the while, his investments will be multiplying, and his business will be thriving.

SECRETS

The King of Coins is a picture of focus. He gazes gently but fixedly at the coin that hovers in front of him. Above his brow is a spark of light, connected to a straight line connected upward to infinity and straight down into the core of everything.

From his heart, an abundance of fresh grains and grasses grow upward to the sky, for he sows, he reaps, and he is a loving and compassionate channel of sustenance and plenty.

If he is not always demonstrative, it is because he is so focused on practical concerns: tending to his fields, managing his investments, and bringing home the treasure upon which his family's fortune can unceasingly thrive.

MEANINGS AND MESSAGES OF KING OF COINS:

- A wealthy, protective fatherly figure has appeared in this situation.
- Invest wisely and diligently tend to your finances.
- Establish a sturdy home base for yourself and others.
- Provide for yourself and others.
- Be a loving bastion of support.
- Be elegant in your minimalism and frugality.
- Take joy in generosity.
- Look at the big picture and take the long view.
- Focus on practical matters and make wise choices that will serve you for decades to come.

MEANINGS AND MESSAGES OF KING OF COINS – REVERSED:

- Someone (maybe you) has temporarily forgotten the joy that can be derived from generously and steadfastly supporting others.

- Don't look for get-rich-quick schemes. Instead, build a sure and steady framework that will nourish your finances over time.
- Put down roots and hold the space for others to feel safe.
- Make responsible choices that will allow you to provide for yourself and others.
- You don't have to be perfect to be a loving bastion of support — through expressing your supportiveness as best you can with what you have, you will find more wisdom and mastery in the process.
- Don't waste money or resources trying to impress others through external measures of status.
- Generosity is a joy. Never wasteful in its true form, it magnetizes more to be generous with.
- Before you decide what to do, zoom out and see the bigger picture and longer view.

Photo © Whitney DeVoto / @devotophoto

ABOUT THE AUTHOR

TESS WHITEHURST blends warmth, wisdom, and wonder into her writing, creating an experience that feels like a conversation with a knowledgeable and empathetic friend. She encourages readers to embrace their uniqueness and guides them toward living more fulfilling, magical lives.

The seven decks and eleven books she's created have been translated into 18 languages and nominated for multiple awards.

Tess has appeared on morning shows on both Fox and NBC, and her feng shui work was featured on the Bravo TV show *Flipping Out*.

Visit Tess, learn about her membership program, read her blog, and sign up for her free newsletter at **TessWhitehurst.com**

ABOUT THE ARTIST

ANA NOVAES, better known as Ltg.Art, is a Brazilian artist based in São Paulo. A professional creator since 2015, Ana uses a mix of techniques including ink, watercolour, gouache, muralism and digital illustration to delve into ancestral myths and stories revealing refreshing perspectives on the feminine. Her raw, soulful aesthetic delivers magic, presence and the melancholy power of sensation and possibility. Be lost in the depth and found in the subtleties of Ana's visionary creations.

Ana's work has been published around the world with Disney, HarperCollins, WOW x WOW, Quarto Group, Fictionz Podcasts and more.

ananovaes.art

ALSO AVAILABLE FROM BLUE ANGEL PUBLISHING®

THE ORACLE OF DAYDREAMS MOONBEAMS
Wisdom and Guidance from Fairytales, Fantasy, and Folklore

Tess Whitehurst
Artwork by Jessica von Braun

Step into the cheeky and enchanting realm of *The Oracle of Daydreams and Moonbeams*. Within these cards lies a tapestry of magic and metaphor inspired by fables, fantasy, and folklore, ready to guide you toward joy and fulfillment.

Like silver slippers and a treasure map, this 46-card oracle deck and guidebook illuminate the yellow brick road to living fully, bravely, and happily. Authored by visionary Tess Whitehurst with charming artwork by Jessica von Braun, each card offers you wisdom and whimsy to navigate life's twists and turns while embracing every precious moment.

As you embark on your personal hero's journey, remember that true transformation lies in the quest itself, not just the destination. Whether outsmarting witches, saving kingdoms, or seeking grails, let this oracle be your companion, supporting you through rainstorms, lost mittens, and uphill climbs — to your own happily-ever-after.

ISBN: 978-1-922574-24-4
46 cards and 128-page color guidebook.

ALSO AVAILABLE FROM BLUE ANGEL PUBLISHING®

THE ANGEL MAGIC ORACLE
Empowering Guidance & Divine Love

Tess Whitehurst
Artwork by Jessica von Braun

Angel magic is accessible to all who seek it. In this ethereal oracle, you have a direct link to the boundless support, insight, and blessings of the celestial realms. Hold the deck to your heart to align yourself with the luminous presence of the angels. Welcome their energy as you shuffle and choose your cards. The big questions and the small ones are received by the angels with love, so you always receive wise, relevant, and practical responses in accord with your highest healing, purpose, and possibility.

Make Every Moment Magic

Angels appear in ways that resonate with our souls and make our consciousness sing. When we are open to their tenderness, we can experience our divinity and know the truth of their guidance through our own awakening.

ISBN: 978-1-922573-93-3
56 cards and 144-page color guidebook.

ALSO AVAILABLE FROM BLUE ANGEL PUBLISHING®

NOVA WITCH TAROT
A deck for curious souls in search of magic

Suki Ferguson
Artwork by Ana Novaes

Weave your unique magic into life's tapestry.

Do you experience life deeply, in all its light and shade? Do you long for a richer understanding of the world and your place in it?

Nova Witch Tarot is a captivating deck tailored for young hearts and those new to tarot. These 78 cards and colour guidebook are your trusted allies, helping you dance through life's twists and turns with empathy and self-love. Illuminate the countless facets of your being while discovering hidden potential and unexpected paths into the future.

ISBN: 978-1-922574-05-3
78 cards and 112-page color guidebook.

ALSO AVAILABLE FROM BLUE ANGEL PUBLISHING®

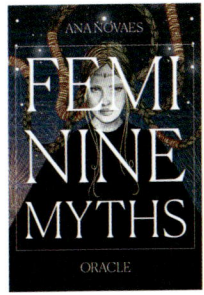

FEMININE MYTHS ORACLE

Ana Novaes

The song of the goddess has echoed since the beginning of time. Now she is here, in her kaleidoscopic expression, to guide you home to your courageous heart.

In this boldly illustrated oracle, feminine deities across many cultures have been uniquely reimagined with a surrealist twist to inspire your multi-faceted gifts. Receive guidance from these all-seeing, shapeshifting beings, who share the mythic stories of ancient Greece, Ireland, Haiti, Yorubaland, Japan and beyond.

Each card's messenger—accompanied by their animal, elemental, celestial and botanical allies—brings primordial wisdom to help you navigate towards the visions of your soul.

Traditional maidens, mothers and crones as well as enigmatic heroines and gender-fluid spirits dance through this deck. Celebrate the many faces, bodies and colors of the feminine, while witnessing your own dynamic beauty and divine potential in their reflection.

ISBN: 978-1-922574-29-9
50 cards and 136-page color guidebook.

NOTES

NOTES

NOTES

NOTES

For more information on this
or any Blue Angel Publishing release,
please visit our website at:

www.BlueAngelOnline.com